The Discursive Construction of the Modern Political Self

This book explores the impact of new media on politicians' construction, presentation, and dissemination of their political selves, focusing on the social media presence of US Representative Alexandria Ocasio-Cortez to offer new insights into the landscape of contemporary political discourse.

Drawing on work from corpus linguistics, interactional sociolinguistics, and critical discourse analysis, Aiello charts the ways in which the politician employed a range of discursive strategies via social media in her first campaign to introduce her political identity to a wider audience, and the subsequent responses by media outlets. The volume examines how she continued to solidify her political agenda throughout the course of her tenure, unpacking her crafting of counterattacks and "clapbacks," in particular, in counteracting delegitimizing attacks from both mainstream media outlets and user-generated content. Aiello brings these insights together to offer a more holistic understanding of American political discourse but also the intersection of language, power, ideology, and the role of social media in modern political campaigns and populist discourses.

The book will be of interest to students and scholars in digital communication, political communication, critical discourse analysis, and sociolinguistics.

Jacqueline Aiello is Assistant Professor at the University of Salerno, Italy. She earned her doctorate in TESOL from New York University. She is the author of *Negotiating Englishes and English-speaking Identities* (2018, Routledge), for which she was awarded the 2019 AIA Junior Book Prize.

Routledge Focus on Linguistics

Understanding Abstract Concepts across Modes in Multimodal Discourse
A Cognitive Linguistic Approach
Elżbieta Górska

Multimodal Theory and Methodology
For the Analysis of (Inter)action and Identity
Sigrid Norris

Linguistic Description in English for Academic Purposes
Helen Basturkmen

Antonyms in Mind and Brain
Evidence from English and German
Sandra Kotzor

Picturing Fiction through Embodied Cognition
Drawn Representations and Viewpoint in Literary Texts
Bien Klomberg, Theresa Schilhab, and Michael Burke

The Discursive Construction of the Modern Political Self
Alexandria Ocasio-Cortez in the Age of Social Media
Jacqueline Aiello

Using AI for Dialoguing with Texts
From Psychology to Cinema and Literature
Yair Neuman, Marcel Danesi and Dan Vilenchik

For more information about this series, please visit: https://www.routledge.com/Routledge-Focus-on-Linguistics/book-series/RFL

The Discursive Construction of the Modern Political Self
Alexandria Ocasio-Cortez in the Age of Social Media

Jacqueline Aiello

NEW YORK AND LONDON

First published 2023
by Routledge
605 Third Avenue, New York, NY 10158

and by Routledge
4 Park Square, Milton Park, Abingdon, Oxon, OX14 4RN

Routledge is an imprint of the Taylor & Francis Group, an informa business

© 2023 Jacqueline Aiello

The right of Jacqueline Aiello to be identified as author of this work has been asserted in accordance with sections 77 and 78 of the Copyright, Designs and Patents Act 1988.

All rights reserved. No part of this book may be reprinted or reproduced or utilised in any form or by any electronic, mechanical, or other means, now known or hereafter invented, including photocopying and recording, or in any information storage or retrieval system, without permission in writing from the publishers.

Trademark notice: Product or corporate names may be trademarks or registered trademarks, and are used only for identification and explanation without intent to infringe.

ISBN: 978-1-032-22569-2 (hbk)
ISBN: 978-1-032-22570-8 (pbk)
ISBN: 978-1-003-27310-3 (ebk)

DOI: 10.4324/9781003273103

Typeset in Times New Roman
by codeMantra

Contents

1 **Introduction**   1
Alexandria Ocasio-Cortez 1
Aims of the book 3
Overarching analytic approaches 4
Contents of the book 6

2 **Modern political discourse: Innovations and revisited traditions**   9
Introduction 9
Political discourse in the post-digital era 9
The language of populism 14

3 **The discursive construction, delegitimization, and defense of political identities**   23
Introduction 23
Constructing (political) selves: positioning, narrative, and coherence 24
Contesting the opposition: delegitimization and recontextualization 27
Taking a stance in the defense of identities 32

4 **"It's time for one of us": The construction of Alexandria Ocasio-Cortez's political self during her first campaign**   38
Introduction 38
The selected viral content of Ocasio-Cortez's first campaign 39
The Courage to Change campaign video 39

The construction of a coherent political self in The
 Courage to Change 41
A tweeted narrative 45
Narrating Alexandria Ocasio-Cortez: novelty and
 populism in her campaign ad and tweets 58

5 **Attacks on a progressive newcomer: Fox News
 coverage and its uptake online** 63
The anti-AOC offensive 63
Methods 64
Dismantling legitimacy on Fox News 67
The recontextualization of Ocasio-Cortez's words
 onto Fox News 77
Fox News coverage of Alexandria Ocasio-Cortez 82
YouTube comments about Fox News coverage 84

6 **"Get used to me slaying": The discursive realization of
 a "clapback queen"** 91
Introduction 91
Data and methods 93
"I am incredibly flattered," "This is not about me:"
 defense, rebuttal, and reprisal on the House floor 95
"Don't hate me cause you ain't me, fellas": expressing
 (dis)alignment on Twitter 102
Conclusions 112

7 **The identity work of a modern leader** 116
Introduction 116
Narrating a new political identity 116
Subverting the narrative 119
Safeguarding the narrative 122
Looking ahead 124

Appendix 129
Index 131

1 Introduction

Alexandria Ocasio-Cortez

The 2016 US Presidential election campaign was like no other. Barack Obama had already artfully used social media in his presidential campaigns, but social media sites became the key battleground sites of the 2016 US presidential race (Buccoliero et al., 2018), through which the most norm-defying discursive practices occurred. These platforms – and Twitter in particular – served as vehicles for Donald Trump to enact his unconventional campaign tactics and develop a "more amateurish" style that strengthened his image as an authentic outsider (Enli, 2017, p. 50). They also served as megaphones through which he broadcast his demagogic claims and publicly berated and debased various minority groups (Milbank, 2015). Trump's unprecedented campaign and subsequent election fueled a growing awareness of a lack of cohesiveness within the American population. Many Americans felt that they were not represented by the president and other elected officials. The chauvinistic, xenophobic, and misogynistic messages that characterized much of his incendiary campaign rhetoric and its widespread coverage gave rise to deep-seated concern over threats to the status and rights of women, people of color, immigrants, Muslims, the disabled, among others under the new administration. What resulted was the inception of a grassroots opposition that took many forms across the nation.

Within this volatile context, the progressive political action committee Justice Democrats set out to "usher in a new generation of diverse working-class Democrats" by recruiting "everyday working Americans" to challenge "out-of-touch" incumbents in primary races (https://justicedemocrats.com/nominate/). In 2017, they recruited 27-year-old Alexandria Ocasio-Cortez for the Democratic primary race for New York's 14th congressional district

DOI: 10.4324/9781003273103-1

(NY-14) seat. Before Ocasio-Cortez announced her candidacy, her opponent Joseph Crowley, monikered "the King of Queens," had run unopposed for more than a decade and was widely heralded as Nancy Pelosi's successor as the next Speaker of the House. Born in the Bronx into a working-class family of Puerto Rican descent in 1989, Ocasio-Cortez resided in the Bronx before moving to the suburbs in Westchester County. She majored in economics and international relations at Boston University and accrued some political experience as an intern in the foreign affairs/immigration constituent office of late Democratic Senator Ted Kennedy and as an organizer on Bernie Sanders' 2016 Presidential election campaign. Her most well-known and frequently cited employment experience before running for the NY-14 seat, however, was tending bar and waiting tables in Manhattan.

Indeed, notwithstanding her political experience, when she released her campaign video titled "The Courage to Change" in May 2018 at just 28 years old, she was largely unknown in the American political landscape. The two-minute video began with the words "Women like me aren't supposed to run for office" and, with these words, crafted carefully to serve as her political debut and introduction, she positioned herself as an antiestablishment candidate not because of her Democratic Socialist political platform, which she described later in the video, but because of who she is: a young, Latina, working-class woman from the Bronx. On 26 June 2018, Ocasio-Cortez shocked the establishment when she unseated her ten-term incumbent opponent and went on to become the youngest Congresswoman in American history.

Since being sworn in as the US Representative for New York's 14th congressional district and the youngest US Congresswoman in American history in January 2019, AOC has claimed the spotlight. Time Magazine dedicated a cover story to her on 1 April 2019 and called her "The Phenom" and "America's lightning rod." With a platform that champions progressive policies and disparages contemporary capitalism, since joining Congress, Ocasio-Cortez has been defined by *Time* magazine as "the second most talked-about politician in America" after Donald Trump, and by the *New York Times* as "the most exposed and fixated-on House freshman in history." She has become a magnetic, polarizing figure in the US political landscape who is at once one of the most visible symbols of left-wing populism and one of the most persistent targets of attacks by the right.

This book explores the construction, presentation, and dissemination of Ocasio-Cortez's political self, with a focus on her social media presence and populist discourses to investigate how she discursively realized her political ascent and to offer new insights into the landscape of contemporary political discourse.

Aims of the book

The present work analyzes the political communication of newcomer politicians through a critical lens that is dedicated to exploring the interrelationship among language, power, and ideology to provide a rich understanding of contemporary political discourse. The book has two overarching aims. First, it investigates the discursive strategies in the political communication of Representative Alexandria Ocasio-Cortez – the most well-known member of the new generation of young American progressivists – and how they have advanced her political agenda and career. Within this first aim, the book first studies content produced by Ocasio-Cortez during her first campaign (2017–2018), including tweets and a campaign video, via Corpus-Assisted Critical Discourse Analysis to unveil the discursive elements and positioning tactics she employed in the effort to construct a political identity and present it to her constituents.

The second aim of this book is to examine via critical discourse analysis opposition attacks levied against the Representative both in mainstream media content and user-generated online content, and the politician's reactions to these attacks across contexts and media. On the one hand, this analysis provides insight into the discursive, semiotic, and multimodal resources and mechanisms deployed in both the criticism directed at Ocasio-Cortez and in her counterattacks – or "clapbacks" – and how they function to undermine (in the former) and defend (in the latter case) her identity, credentials, and agenda. On the other hand, the study of these attacks and their rebuttal creates a juxtaposition of divergent political discourses – including left- and right-wing populist discourses – to arrive at a more holistic understanding of communication within the contemporary American political landscape, in general, and populism, in particular. This section of the book seeks to unveil the ways in which her own narrative and modes of expression have evolved over time and as her role shifted from unknown newcomer to political powerhouse.

Although much has been written in the past five years about the changing political landscape of the United States, there are several pivotal ways in which this book differs from existing literature.

4 *Introduction*

This book's focus on Representative Ocasio-Cortez and its methodological approach is innovative and results in more granularity in different respects. By centering on the communication produced by and about a renowned social actor in the years immediately preceding and following her shocking Congressional win, this work provides readers with a nuanced understanding of the construction, projection, and defense of the political identity of a popular, magnetic, and polarizing figure in the US political landscape who, as a result of her sudden rise and far-reaching influence, has served and will continue serve as a communicative model for current and future politicians.

Furthermore, most recent work has centered on Donald Trump as an antiestablishment political newcomer and on right-wing populism. The concern of the present book with a Representative who can be defined as a left-wing populist serving as the political opposition to the 45th US President sheds new light on the American political landscape, in general, and, in particular, it offers novel insights into the American vein of left-wing populist discourse, into how right-wing populist users discursively position the ideological opposition, and into the similarities and differences in the strategies used in left- and right-wing populist discourse. Next, other work has been dedicated to Ocasio-Cortez, but this book's use of data drawn across media outlets (including both mainstream media coverage of and user-generated responses to the politician) and genres of media (including textual tweets, images and screenshots, and campaign videos) foregrounds social media communication and allows a more ecological approach to the modern media environment. Additionally, the support of innovative approaches including multimodal critical discourse analysis and interactional sociolinguistic analysis casts light on intentionality, intersubjectivity, indexicality, (de)legitimization, and ultimately the articulation of agency.

Overarching analytic approaches

Critical discourse analysis

Critical Discourse Analysis (CDA)[1] attempts to capture the interrelationship between language, power, and ideology. It is primarily concerned with studying "the way social power abuse, dominance, and inequality are enacted, reproduced, and resisted by text and talk in the social and political context" (van Dijk, 2005, p. 352). Of the many critical approaches that can be incorporated under the heading CDA, which have been associated with the seminal work of scholars such as Jim Gee, Norman Fairclough, Teun van Dijk, Ruth Wodak, critical discourse analysts agree that language is a social practice and that the context of language use is critical (Wodak, 2001). As Fuchs (2018) asserts, "a comprehensive definition of CDA is that it critically analyses and theorises *texts* in their *contexts* in order to advance the *prospect*s for progressive changes in society" (p. 200).

Fairclough (1989) explained that discourse analysis involves not only attention to processes of production and interpretation but also "the relationship between texts, processes, and the social conditions, both the immediate conditions of the situational context and the more remote conditions of institutional and social structures" (p. 26). The Discourse-Historical Approach (DHA), one of the most prominent critical approaches to the study of discourse that stresses the importance of anchoring discourses and texts to their historical context (Riesigl & Wodak, 2001; 2009), identifies three dimensions within texts: the topics, the discursive strategies used, and the linguistic means used to realize topics and strategies (Wodak, 2011). The discursive strategies in the DHA are nomination, predication, argumentation, perspectivization, and mitigation and intensification that can be explored by answering the following questions, respectively (Riesigl, 2018, p. 52):

- How are persons, objects, phenomena, events, processes, and actions named and referred to linguistically in the discourse in question?
- What characteristics or qualities are attributed to social actors, objects, phenomena, events, processes, and actions mentioned in the discourse?
- What arguments are employed in discourse?
- From what perspective are these nominations, attributions, and arguments expressed?
- Are the respective utterances articulated overtly, are they intensified or mitigated?

The DHA also takes the following four dimensions of context into account (Riesigl, 2018, p. 53):

- The immediate co-text and co-discourse
- The intertextual and interdiscursive relationship between utterances, texts, genres, and discourses

6 *Introduction*

- Social factors and institutional frames of a specific context of situation
- The wider sociopolitical and historical context

By considering these four layers, discourse analysts who follow this approach can "explore how discourses, genres and texts change due to socio-political contexts" (Wodak, 2011, p. 39). As Riesigl (2018) notes, since today's world is characterized by "a series of far-reaching social, political, economic and ecological changes," change is a "basic historical category," and discourse is relevant to all of these changes, the Discourse-Historical Approach is perfectly suited to study the contemporary world (p. 59).

Corpus-assisted discourse studies

Partington (2010) defines the principal endeavor of Corpus-Assisted Discourse Studies (CADS) as "the investigation and comparison of features of particular discourse types, integrating into the analysis, where appropriate, techniques and tools developed within corpus linguistics" (p. 88). The aim of CADS is to combine quantitative approaches to the analysis of large numbers of tokens within a corpus with qualitative discourse analytical approaches to unveil non-obvious meanings unnoticeable to the naked eye (Partington, 2010; Partington, Duguid & Taylor, 2013). Corpus-driven approaches, in particular, intend to reduce the assumptions that researchers bring to the text or discourses and to develop a comprehensive description of the corpus (Tognini-Bonelli, 2001). By applying these approaches, it is possible to make "more credible interpretations based on salient linguistic patterns in large amounts of data that may otherwise have been overlooked" (Subtirelu & Baker, 2018, p. 118).

Contents of the book

This introduction provided an overview of Alexandria Ocasio-Cortez, the main actor on which this book pivots, as well as the book's aims, and its analytic approaches. Chapter 2 traces, in broad strokes, the ways in which new media and populism have affected modern political discourse, and Chapter 3 provides the overarching theoretical frameworks that underpin the investigation into the language used by and against the politician. Chapters 4–6 each cover one of the three main perspectives of the book, or the realization, reception, and defense of Ocasio-Cortez's political identity. First, Chapter 4 charts the ways in which Ocasio-Cortez employed a range of discursive strategies in her first campaign to narrate her political identity to a wider audience as an electable candidate for the US House of Representatives, particularly in her campaign advertisement and her tweets. Second, Chapter 5 turns to the responses by media outlets by examining the delegitimating account told within Fox News coverage of the Representative. Third, Chapter 6 relates how Ocasio-Cortez articulated her rebuttal, unpacking her crafting of counterattacks and "clapbacks," in particular, in counteracting delegitimizing attacks from both mainstream media outlets and user-generated content. Chapter 7 concludes the book with a discussion that brings together these insights and summarizes the broader lessons learned from examining Ocasio-Cortez's political discourse at intersection of language, power, ideology, and the role of social media.

Note

1 Critical Discourse Studies (CDS) is becoming the preferred acronym to include studies with philosophical, theoretical, methodological and practical emphases rather than applied analysis (Flowerdew & Richardson, 2018). Because the present book focuses on analysis, CDA is used here.

References

Buccoliero, L., Bellio, E., Crestini, G., & Arkoudas, A. (2018). Twitter and politics: Evidence from the US presidential elections 2016. *Journal of Marketing Communications,* 26(1), 1–27.
Enli, G. (2017). Twitter as arena for the authentic outsider: Exploring the social media campaigns of Trump and Clinton in the 2016 US presidential election. *European Journal of Communication,* 32(1), 50–61.
Fairclough, N. (1989). *Language and Power.* New York: Longman.
Flowerdew, J. & Richardson, J.E. (2018). Introduction. In J. Flowerdew & J.E. Richardson (Eds.). *The Routledge Handbook of Critical Discourse Studies* (pp. 1–10). London-New York: Routledge.
Fuchs, C. (2018). *Digital Demagogue: Authoritarian Capitalism in the Age of Trump and Twitter.* London: Pluto Press.
Milbank, D. (2015, December 1). Donald Trump is a bigot and a racist, *Washington Post,* Retrieved from https://www.washingtonpost.com/opinions/donald-trump-is-a-bigot-and-a-racist/2015/12/01/a2a47b96-9872-11e5-8917-653b65c809eb_story.html?utm_term=.5de1a471d790

Partington, A., (2010). Modern diachronic corpus-assisted discourse studies (MD-CADS) on UK newspapers: An overview of the project. *Corpora*, 5(2), 83–108.
Partington, A., Duguid, A., & Taylor, C. (2013). *Patterns and Meanings in Discourse: Theory and Practice in Corpus-Assisted Discourse Studies (CADS)*. Amsterdam: Benjamins.
Riesigl, M. (2018). The discourse-historical approach. In J. Flowerdew & J.E. Richardson (Eds.). *The Routledge Handbook of Critical Discourse Studies* (pp. 44–59). London-New York: Routledge.
Riesigl, M. & Wodak, R. (2009). The discourse-historical approach (DHA). In R. Wodak &M. Meyer (Eds.). *Methods for Critical Discourse Analysis* (pp. 87–121). London: Sage.
Riesigl, M. & Wodak, R. (2001). *Discourse and Discrimination*. London-New York: Routledge.
Subtirelu, N.C. & Baker, P. (2018). Corpus-based approaches. In J. Flowerdew & J.E. Richardson (Eds.). *The Routledge Handbook of Critical Discourse Studies* (pp. 106–119). London-New York: Routledge.
Tognini-Bonelli, E. (2001). *Corpus Linguistics at Work*. Amsterdam: Benjamins.
van Dijk, T. (2005). Critical discourse analysis. In D. Schiffrin, D. Tannen, & H.E. Hamilton (Eds.). *The Handbook of Discourse Analysis* (pp. 352–371). Malden, MA: Blackwell Publishers Ltd.
Wodak, R. (2011). *The Discourse of Politics in Action: 'Politics as Usual'* (2nd ed.). Basingstoke: Palgrave Macmillan.
Wodak, R. (2001). What CDA is about - A summary of its history, important concepts and its developments. In R. Wodak & M. Meyer (Eds.). *Methods of Critical Discourse Analysis* (pp. 1–13). London-Thousand Oaks: SAGE.

2 Modern political discourse
Innovations and revisited traditions

Introduction

A lot has been written about new media and populism in the past decades, and an in-depth overview of these concepts is beyond the scope of this book. Instead, this chapter intends to contextualize the political discourse discussed in the present work through the lenses of new media and populism, which have transformed the ways that politicians have constructed, presented, and disseminated their political selves and their relationships with their constituents and their opponents. It, therefore, traces, in broad strokes, how they have emerged, what they mean for political communication, and how they have affected modern political discourse while taking a closer look at specific elements relevant to the present book, or political campaign advertisements, political tweets, and the Fox News brand of populism.

Political discourse in the post-digital era

Renowned sociolinguist Jan Blommaert (2020) theorized that we live in a post-digital era in which the notions of traditional political discourse as originating from professional politicians alone, the sharply outlined distinction between online and offline domains, and the public as a homogenous entity are no longer valid. Instead, models of communication are affected by a new hybrid media system, the online–offline nexus, and a fragmented public sphere. Today, complex structures of communication convey political discourse. The direct line between a politician and the public has been in some ways strengthened and, in others, interrupted and even entirely cut off. Political discourse does not reach the public straight from the mouths of politicians or mainstream media reporters alone. People's understandings of this discourse are influenced by the "new kinds of communicative economies (including resources, actors, and relationships between actors)" afforded by digital spaces (Blommaert, 2020). While in a sense these immeasurable changes to communication structures pit politicians against other members of the public for political space and attention, the advent of online media has provided vast resources to political actors. New media provide political candidates with crucial vehicles during election season through which they can have unmediated access to the masses for self-promotion and voter mobilization. By making communication (seem) more direct, they have occasioned a significant shift in the relationship among candidates, reporters, and voters. Candidates can circumvent the press in conveying their message to voters, and voters interested in learning about candidates can do so without an intermediary, by visiting their social media sites. Through social media, politicians can strategically orchestrate their public and private roles, project themselves in a positive light, and add a level of political personalization and intimacy with their constituents (Enli & Skogerbø, 2013; Kruikemeier, 2014). They also provide politicians with valuable feedback both via their interactive channels and unfettered access to voters, and via their metrics (followers, shares, and likes) through which they can measure their popularity.

This book is specifically concerned with how online media are employed by politicians in the construction, negotiation, and defense of their political image. These platforms have revolutionized the way in which political communication occurs both by embedding traditional vehicles of political messaging and by proposing new modes of communication. The next subsections take a closer look at two types of political messaging often used by politicians today that fall into each of these categories, or political advertisements and tweets.

Revisiting political campaign advertisements

Political advertisements combine multiple semiotic modes including images, writing, layout, speech, gesture, and sound (Meade & Robles, 2017). Mackay (2013) identifies political ads as a genre with a series of expected features including length (usually between 30 seconds and 2 minutes), self-legitimization and/or other-delegitimization, the use of "politically relevant" material, and the required statement that specifies the identity of the candidate (or special interest group) and declares that the message has been approved by them (p. 349).

For decades, American politicians have relied on campaign ads in their effort to sway voters in their favor. As detailed by Iyengar (2011), candidates have successfully manipulated the media into covering their candidacies and platforms by making ads with distorted or false information. A new approach to campaign coverage that pushed back against and criticized misleading ads did little to dissuade this practice. It instead encouraged some candidates to develop ads that would intentionally bring forth this coverage, in keeping with the adage "all press is good press" (Iyengar, 2011). Thus, political ads have been used not only as overt tools for candidate promotion during the campaign season, but they have also been employed to steer press coverage in desirable directions.

Campaign ads have a well-established tradition in the promotion of candidates, and they have long been the subject of analysis. More recent work in this vein has explored how legitimization is achieved through this form of political messaging. For instance, Mackay (2013) applied CDA to analyze three ads produced by Obama's camp in the 2008 US presidential campaign and found that multimodality played a key role in the legitimization of the candidate. More recently, with a focus on ads produced by Bernie Sanders in the 2020 US presidential election, Schubert (2021) illustrates how multimodal cohesion served as a rhetorical technique in the persuasive discourse of campaign advertising that foregrounded the candidate, legitimized his political agenda, and created an "us versus them" binary in which adversaries were delegitimized. This research has been pivotal in broadening our understandings of multimodal forms of political discourse and of how this genre has been adopted and adapted within today's post-digital era.

Today, of course, political ads are no longer relegated to the realm of television. New media have created a digital politics landscape that has significantly altered the distribution and form of political ads. This technology grants voters the possibility "to bypass or supplement media treatment of the campaign" and "take matters into their own hands" by engaging directly with online content (Iyengar, 2011, p. 5). In fact, as explained by Mackay (2013), "a candidate can now have their own 'channel' onto which hours and hours of material may be placed, framed, (internally) commented upon and analyzed (the channel itself becoming one big political ad)" (p. 351). For a fraction of the price, web-only ads satisfy the public's demand to "hear it straight from the horse's mouth" (Mackay, 2013, p. 351).

Video sharing site YouTube and similar platforms make it possible for viewers to engage directly with the campaign ads, by commenting and sharing the ad with their network. Barack Obama's first presidential campaign broke new ground in its use of online communication, with YouTube playing a significant role in the dissemination of campaign messages and ads (Iyengar, 2011; Mackay, 2013). Another major change in political campaign ads occurred in 2017, after the 2016 presidential election. At this time, a new kind of campaign ad was generated in "response to the carefully contrived, quickly digestible personas presented in traditional campaign ads" (Goldstein, 2019, online). Alexandria Ocasio-Cortez's first campaign ad embodied this new subgenre. *The Courage to Change*, released in May 2018 and produced by media company Means of Production, featured a voice-over that Ocasio-Cortez wrote and delivered herself. Its documentary-like style aimed to convey authenticity and intimacy with her viewers. This format proved to be effective. Ocasio-Cortez's campaign ad was a viral phenomenon that became the most-watched political campaign video of the season (Watkins, 2019). The novelty of its form as well as its viral status render this content worthy of investigation as a distinctive vehicle through which the candidate constructed her political self and introduced it to her constituents, which is one of the aims of Chapter 4.

Political tweets

Twitter has come to play a particularly pivotal role in contemporary politics with political tweets increasingly assuming a central role in political communication. Like political ads, Twitter has served as a platform for politicians to both broadcast their message and maneuver mainstream news coverage. Twitter, however, contains unique features that make it particularly attractive for politicians. Duncombe (2019) argues that it comes down to its structure: politicians can author brief, easily scanned, and tracked messages (tweets) that are addressed to their constituents and/or to other politicians but are broadcast to a much wider audience. A key component of Twitter, Duncombe (2019) adds, is that it is at once egalitarian for its open and dynamic communication (e.g., any Twitter user can @mention another) and hierarchical like offline communication (e.g., tweets and mentions can be ignored; a Twitter user can follow another user with no reciprocation).

Buccoliero et al. (2018) argue that the rise of Twitter "signaled a change in politics as profound as the one which occurred in 1960 when John F. Kennedy showed the effectiveness of television as a campaign tool" (p. 92). The significance and widespread use of Twitter for political communication has resulted in a rapidly expanding body of research on the topic. Jungherr (2016) centers on research on Twitter use during election campaigns with a comprehensive literature review of 127 studies to disclose, among other things, the variables that predicted the adoption of Twitter among political candidates (e.g., Twitter users were more likely to be members of the opposition party, young politicians, and in urban settings), how candidates and parties used Twitter (e.g., it was mainly used to share campaign information and links to their own websites), and the effects of tweets on users (e.g., tweets engendered greater feelings of connectedness than traditional modes of communication).

Scores of studies have analyzed Twitter use in the American political realm since the 2016 US presidential campaign, with most of the attention directed to Donald Trump. Trump's Twitter feed may have been halted when his account was famously suspended from the platform in 2021, but it has been and continues to be a contentious object of discussion. In Enli (2017), who argued that Twitter made it possible for Trump to come across as a viable candidate, the juxtaposition of Hillary Clinton's more professional Twitter use against Trump's amateur, authentic style during the 2016 presidential campaign evidenced a trend of de-professionalization in political communication. Ott (2017) uses Trump's Twitter feed as a case study to demonstrate how the platform privileges simple, impulsive, and uncivil (political) discourse. Fuchs (2018) applies CDA to a sample of Donald Trump's tweets to display how he used nationalist slogans, created "us versus them" binaries, disseminated disinformation, and used multimodal resources on the platform. He argues that "Twitter's brevity, speed, individualism and its structure for the accumulation of acclamation (via 'likes' and 'retweets') supports Trump's use of it as a communication tool for authoritarian leadership" (p. 250). These studies have delved deep into Trump's demagogic yet skillful Twitter use that retained the media's attention and secured free propaganda for the Trump brand, and they have provided fruitful insights into how political communication occurs by means of this social media platform (Fuchs, 2018).

The present work turns the spotlight onto Ocasio-Cortez's Twitter use. Also acclaimed for her expert use of and impressive following on social media, in January 2019, Ocasio-Cortez was tasked by the House Democratic Policy and Communications Committee to brief her partisan colleagues "on the most effective ways to engage constituents on Twitter and the importance of digital storytelling," as US Today reported. That same article defined Ocasio-Cortez as "a social media star" and a Mashable article that reported on that briefing captioned a picture of the Representative "Alexandria Ocasio-Cortez, queen of Twitter." At the time, the same month that she took office, her @AOC account had amassed 2.42 million followers (Collins, 2019). By May 2022, this number rose fivefold to 13 million followers.

While much has been written about Trump's Twitter use, there is to date a dearth of research on the use of the platform by the "queen of Twitter." Yet, many have attributed Ocasio-Cortez's success and popularity to her masterful use of social media, so an exploration into how she has used the platform is warranted. Thus, Ocasio-Cortez's tweets have been selected as a primary subject of study in the present book.

The language of populism

In the preface to his classic discussion of populism, Laclau (2005) argues that "populism has no referential unity because it is ascribed not to a delimitable phenomenon but to a social logic whose effects cut across many phenomena" (p. xi). Populist politics simplifies political space and aims to turn diverse grievances and demands of "the people" into a unified, equivalential articulation of demands (Laclau, 2005; Laclau & Mouffe, 2001). Populist leaders and movements depend on "empty signifiers," "or symbols that lack particular referents and thus can represent the diversity of specific demands and of 'the people' as a whole" (Hallin, 2021, p. 51), in their construction of a simplified popular identity out of a plurality of demands (Panizza & Stavrakakis, 2021). Unlike other approaches to populism, Laclau's (2005) conceptualization does not pigeonhole "the people" as a one-dimensional and unempirical given (Kranert, 2020). This is critical because the constructed character of "the people" is one of the most fruitful areas of exploration within populism and its discourses.

In *The Populist Persuasion: An American History*, historian Michael Kazin (2017) outlines the evolution of populisms in the American context since the Revolution. The founding of the United States was indisputably fraught with suspicion of authority and from its inception American democracy has been "grounded in the wisdom of common, productive folk set apart from, and often against, the corruptions of privilege and power" (Wells & Rochefort, 2021, p. 346). "The people" is a concept inscribed at the start of the founding document of the nation, as "We the people" opens the Preamble to the US Constitution, ratified in 1788. With this opening, the founding fathers appealed to an ideal collective of American citizens, but its understanding was likely restricted to the identities of the authors: white, male, and well-to-do. From the start of the nineteenth century onward, "the people" acquired a more specific denotation rooted in Jeffersonianism and bound to producerism, "an ethic, a moral conviction" that held that "only those who created wealth in tangible, material ways (on and under the land, in workshops, on the sea) could be trusted to guard the nation's piety and liberties" (Kazin, 2017, p. 13). Thus, "the people" were producers who adhered to the Protestant work ethic, did necessary societal work, created wealth with their manual labor, relied on their own efforts, and were traditionally bound to masculinity.

This group can be traced to the first official American "Populists" – late-nineteenth-century farmers who felt their independence and old order threatened by powerful, politically backed institutions (McMath, 1993) – whose movement coalesced into the People's Party. Kazin (2017) argues that the People's Party can be linked to one of two types of American populism prevalent in today's American political landscape, often labeled "left-wing" populism and associated with Bernie Sanders and, as will be argued in Chapter 4, Alexandria Ocasio-Cortez. In this populist tradition, the conception of "the people" is based primarily on economic terms and the antagonistic "other" is defined exclusively "upward" or "at corporate elites and their enablers in government who have allegedly betrayed the interests of the men and women who do the nation's essential work" (Kazin, 2017, p. xiii).

Donald Trump may have thrown the second type of contemporary American populism, or "right-wing" populism, into relief, but it is deeply rooted in American history, with proponents such as Andrew Jackson, Father Coughlin, and the Ku Klux Klan. This populist tradition also inculpates elites for threatening the well-being of "the common folk," but their understanding of "the people" is much narrower and, oftentimes, ethnically restrictive, constituted, for most of American history, by "real" Americans who are white and of European heritage (Kazin, 2017, p. xiv). This type of populism can be defined as "racial nationalism" that typically alleges that there is "a nefarious alliance between evil forces on high and the unworthy, dark-skinned poor below—a cabal that imperils the interests and values of the patriotic (white) majority in the middle" (p. xiv). This brief discussion that has zeroed in on American populist traditions and recent manifestations has shown that populism is dynamic and evanescent, and it has well-established foundations in American history. "From the birth of the United States to the present day," Kazin (2017) argues, "images of conflict between the powerful and the powerless have run through our civic life, filling it with discord and meaning" (p. 1). Clashes between small farmers and financiers, between workers and industrialists, between God-fearing families and federal bureaucrats have been instanced in political discourse and political campaigns throughout American history. Wells and Rochefort (2021) declare:

> Populism's foremost defining characteristic, its anti-elitism – its sense that some set of 'genuine' people are suffering at the hands of a (variously defined) set of economic, political, or cultural elites – is to be found throughout the country's history, across its political spectrum, and in every campaign season.
>
> (p. 345)

Kazin (2017) adds that politicians at both ends of the political spectrum have run campaigns based on the promise to fight for "the people" against a wide array of oppressors, and that this imagery lies at the heart of "the language of populism":

> Whether orated, written, drawn, broadcast, or televised, this language is used by those who claim to speak for the vast majority of Americans who work hard and love their country. That is the most basic and telling definition of populism: a language whose speakers conceive of ordinary people as a noble assemblage not bounded narrowly by class, view their elite opponents as self-serving and undemocratic, and seek to mobilize the former against the latter.
>
> (p. 1)

Thus, populism is a language in which American politicians have been well versed since the country's inception.

Conceptualizing populism as a language is very useful when considering its analysis. In fact, Laclau (2005) included discourse and rhetoric as two of the three categories central to his theoretical approach to populism (pp. 68–72). More directly, Ostiguy (2017) stresses that populism "can only be studied through discourse" (p. 74). It is not surprising, therefore, that the language that has produced and spread populism has been analyzed, most fruitfully with (critical) discourse analysis. Two recent volumes that collect research studies that explore "discourse" in their effort to comprehend the populist phenomenon are particularly insightful: *Discursive Approaches to Populism Across Disciplines* (Kranert, 2020), and *Populism in Global Perspective: A Performative and Discursive Approach* (Ostiguy, Panizza & Moffitt, 2021). These volumes engage in populist discourses created at both ends of the political spectrum, within different global regions, and using different media. Many of these studies apply CDA, since examinations of the "us" versus "them" constructions typical of populism sit well within this approach, and it facilitates investigations into the meanings of "the people," "the elite," and the aims of the populisms analyzed.

This book aims to build on this preceding work with a focus on language, which is central to politics, in general, and populism, in particular (Kranert, 2020). The understanding of populism adopted in this book is influenced by Laclau's (2005) theorizations and rooted in Kazin's (2017) historical overview, but it is broad to encompass several strands and perspectives including the left-wing populist discourse crafted by Ocasio-Cortez in her first campaign, and the right-wing populist discourse of American conservative cable network Fox News.

The populisms of Fox News

Launched in 1996 to cater to conservative viewers, Fox News has distinguished itself from other cable news networks since its onset. It was pioneering in its creation of a format that has prioritized news-talk shows and emotionally expressive and tabloid-style politics over detached and professionally neutral news reporting (Peck, 2014; Wells & Rochefort, 2021). Its aesthetic and format serve to bolster a primary populist narrative crafted by the network: there are two rival media systems constituted by the people-focused Fox News and the elite-focused journalistic establishment (Peck, 2021). Fox News hosts often aim to show that their news analyses are biased in favor of "the people" because they want to show that they are working in the interests of ordinary Americans (Peck, 2019). In doing so, Fox News presents itself as the voice of "ordinary Americans" (Peck, 2014; 2019).

Peck's (2014; 2019; 2021) scholarship has been pivotal in tracing the ways in which Fox News has crafted and employed populist discourses. He has argued that Fox News employs populist terms to address its audience, including "the folks" and "middle America" which "thread and 'articulate' the various political issues of the conservative movement – gun rights, pro-life, deregulation – on what Laclau terms a 'chain of equivalence'" (p. 163). This "equivalential logic" makes it possible for the network to "symbolically condense the myriad of factions and interest groups that comprise any given political movement into one unitary bloc" (Peck, 2021, p. 163). The "Fox" versus "mainstream media" dichotomy is, in fact, only one of the populist narratives created by the network. The network also establishes a producerism-driven dichotomy of "over-educated elites" versus "producing Americans" (Peck, 2019). When he was president, Fox offered another narrative based on Donald Trump and his adversaries by providing receptive, supportive coverage that imparted triumphant tales and constant acclaim of the former president and made vehement attacks against his opponents (Tumber & Waisbord, 2021).

Peck (2019) has advanced the theory that Fox News has appropriated the discourse of cultural populism, or a political discourse that "champions the common wisdom, taste, and intellectual capacities of everyday people, and denounces justifications for power based on credentials and elite cultural knowledge" (p. 127). One way in which this strategy is enacted is by appealing to "'lowbrow' cultural forms (e.g. NASCAR), lifestyle practices (e.g. shopping at Walmart), and aesthetics (e.g. hyper-patriotic graphics, bleach-blonde anchors)" (Peck, 2021, p. 163). A second aspect of this strategy "involves performing an affinity with lay epistemic culture" (Peck, 2021, p. 163). Fox hosts and anchors strive to embody the cultural–epistemological disposition of the demographic majority of the network audience: non-college-educated viewers. They emphasize their concern and outrage and gloss over expertise, credentials, and empirical support of their claims (Peck, 2021).

Fox News personalities have, in fact, come to be known as exponents of populist rhetoric. One such example is Tucker Carlson, whose primetime Fox News show "Tucker Carlson Tonight" became the highest-rated program in cable news history in 2020, tallying an average of 4.33 million nightly viewers (Concha, 2020). Although Carlson himself has resisted the populist label (MacDougald, 2019), its appropriateness is undeniable when perusing his 2018 book *Ship of Fools: How a Selfish Ruling Class is Bringing America to the Brink of Revolution*, a New York Times bestseller. In the book, as the title of the work suggests, Carlson offers an unflattering account of the American ruling elite. The introduction to the book presents a biting critique of the nation's elite ruling class that cuts across major party lines. He describes "selfish and unwise leaders" who made "decades of selfish and unwise decisions" (p. 3), and later adds: "our new ruling class doesn't care, not simply about American citizens, but about the future of the country itself" (pp. 14–15). These trenchant attacks constitute one of the key elements of populist rhetoric: vilifying "the elite" (the ruling class) for not safeguarding the well-being of the people (American citizens) and, by extension, for going against the interests of the nation. Evidence of a horizontal exclusion between "the people" and "dangerous others" embedded within a nationalist and xenophobic ideology also emerges in the introduction to Carlson's book. Carlson (2018) charges that illegal immigrants fundamentally altered the fabric of the United States, "a nation that was overwhelmingly European, Christian, and English-speaking fifty years ago" (p. 10) and paints a glib future scenario in which the predicted replacement of low-skilled jobs by automation results in unemployed, "angry and disenfranchised" immigrants. "Things could get volatile," he warns (p. 11). Thus, the welfare of an ethnically defined "people" (a subgroup constituted by "European, Christian, and English-speaking" Americans) is threatened by "dangerous others" ("illegal" immigrants) whose arrival is facilitated by the elite (policy- and lawmakers). It is unsurprising that this populist rhetoric makes its way into Fox News programming, and particularly in his show "Tucker Carlson Tonight".

The Fox News formula that features emotionally charged opinions over neutral coverage, champions "ordinary Americans" at the expense of impartiality, and advances populist narratives has proven successful. According to the Pew Research Center, Republicans trust Fox News more than any other news outlet. In 2021, Fox News Channel was the most-watched cable network for the sixth consecutive year and the highest-rated US cable news outlet for the 20th consecutive year, according to Nielsen Media Research data (Mastrangelo, 2022). In the present book, this network was, thus, chosen as a provider of sources of political opposition with respect to Representative Ocasio-Cortez (discussed in Chapter 5) not only because of its right-wing populist rhetoric but also because of its widespread reach and influence.

A discussion of the language of contemporary populism is incomplete without consideration of one of its most propitious spaces, or social media. Here, the two main areas of interest of the present chapter coalesce. Social media's ability to give a platform for the previously marginalized and to draw together an otherwise dispersed people has led to the advancement of populist movements. Gerbauldo (2018) has argued that social media have become a channel for populist appeals because they serve as "a platform for the voice of the people in opposition to the mainstream news media, accused of being in cahoots with the financial and political establishment" (p. 749). As suggested earlier, recent work on political communication has focused on the use of social media as a communicative platform for prominent populist politicians, not least Donald Trump. The present work examines not only the social media communication written and shared by Ocasio-Cortez, but it also takes into account the affordances provided by these platforms – and specifically YouTube – to investigate how users engaged with the populist messages within uploaded Fox News segments. Thus, with heed to the innovations and revisited traditions discussed in this chapter, the present book studies the juxtaposition of different genres, media, and modes of divergent political discourses – including left- and right-wing populist discourses – to arrive at a more holistic understanding of political communication within the contemporary American, post-digital political landscape.

References

Blommaert, J. (2020). Political discourse in post-digital societies. *Trabalhos em Linguística Aplicada*, 59(1), 390–403.

Buccoliero, L., Bellio, E., Crestini, G., & Arkoudas, A. (2018). Twitter and politics: Evidence from the US presidential elections 2016. *Journal of Marketing Communications*, 26(1), 1–27.

Carlson, T. (2018). *Ship of Fools: How a Selfish Ruling Class is Bringing America to the Brink of Revolution*. New York: Free Press.

Collins, E. (2019). Alexandria Ocasio-Cortez, a social media star, to school House Democrats on Twitter use *USA Today*, Retrieved from: https://eu.usatoday.com/story/news/politics/2019/01/16/alexandria-ocasio-cortez-lawmakers-tap-new-members-twitter-expertise/2592539002/

Concha, J. (1 July 2020). Trump dings CNN, 'Morning Joe' ratings as Tucker Carlson sets record. *The Hill*, Retrieved 27 April 2022, https://thehill.com/homenews/media/505386-trump-dings-cnn-morning-joe-ratings-as-tucker-carlson-sets-record/

Duncombe, C. (2019). The politics of Twitter: Emotions and the power of social media. *International Political Sociology*, 13(4), 409–429.
Enli, G. (2017). Twitter as arena for the authentic outsider. *European Journal of Communication*, 32(1), 50–61.
Enli, G.S. & Skogerbø, E. (2013). Personalized campaigns in party-centred politics. *Information, Communication & Society*, 16(5), 757–774.
Fuchs, C. (2018). *Digital Demagogue: Authoritarian Capitalism in the Age of Trump and Twitter*. London: Pluto Press.
Gerbauldo, P. (2018). Social media and populism: An elective affinity? *Media, Culture & Society*, 40(5), 745–753.
Goldstein, A. (2019). Anatomy of the cinematic profile: What does it take to make viral political ads? *Medium*, Retrieved from: https://medium.com/digital-brand-management/anatomy-of-the-cinematic-profile-what-does-it-take-to-make-viral-political-ads-82e360ded895
Hallin, D.C. (2021). Rethinking mediatisation: Populism and the mediatisation of politics. In H. Tumber & S. Waisbord (Eds.), *The Routledge Companion to Media Disinformation and Populism* (pp. 49–58). London-New York: Routledge.
Iyengar, S. (2011). The media game: New moves, old strategies. *The Forum*, 9(1), 1–6.
Jungherr, A. (2016). Twitter use in election campaigns: A systematic literature review. *Journal of Information Technology & Politics*, 13(1), 72–91.
Kazin, M. (2017). *The Populist Persuasion: An American History*. Ithaca-London: Cornell University Press.
Kranert, M. (2020). *Discursive Approaches to Populism Across Disciplines*. Cham: Palgrave MacMillan.
Kruikemeier, S. (2014). How political candidates use Twitter and the impact on votes. *Computers in Human Behavior*, 34, 131–139.
Laclau, E. (2005). *On Populist Reason*. London-New York: Verso.
Laclau, E. & Mouffe, C. (2001). *Hegemony and Socialist Strategy* (2nd ed.). London: Verso.
MacDougald, P. (2019). Is Tucker Carlson the most important pundit in America? *New York Magazine*, Retrieved from: http://nymag.com/intelligencer/2019/09/is-tucker-carlson-the-most-important-pundit-in-america.html
Mackay, R.R. (2013). Multimodal legitimation: Looking at and listening to Obama's ads. In P. Cap & U. Okulska (Eds.), *Analyzing Genres in Political Communication: Theory and Practice* (pp. 345–377). Amsterdam-Philadelphia: John Benjamins.
Mastrangelo, D. (2022). Fox News tops yearly ratings for 20th consecutive year, *The Hill*, Retrieved from: https://thehill.com/homenews/media/-592316-fox-news-tops-yearly-ratings-for-20th-consecutive-year
McMath, R.C. (1993). *American Populism: A Social History 1877–1898*. New York: Hill and Wang.
Meade, M. & Robles, J. (2017). Historical and existential coherence in political commercials. *Discourse & Communication*, 11(4), 404–432.

Ostiguy, P. (2017). Populism: A socio-cultural approach. In R. Kaltwasser, et al. (Eds.), *The Oxford Handbook of Populism* (pp. 73–97). Oxford: Oxford University Press.

Ostiguy, P., Panizza, F., & Moffitt, B. (Eds.). (2021). *Populism in Global Perspective*. New York-London: Routledge.

Ott, B.L. (2017). The age of Twitter: Donald J. Trump and the politics of debasement. *Critical Studies in Media Communication*, 34 (1), pp. 59–68.

Panizza, F. & Stavrakakis, Y. (2021). Populism, hegemony, and the political construction of "The People". In P. Ostiguy, F. Panizza & B. Moffitt (Eds.), *Populism in Global Perspective* (pp. 21–46). New York-London: Routledge.

Peck, R. (2021). 'Listen to your gut': How Fox News's populist style changed the American public sphere and journalistic truth in the process. In H. Tumber & S. Waisbord (Eds.), *The Routledge Companion to Media Disinformation and Populism* (pp. 160–168). London-New York: Routledge.

Peck, R. (2019). *Fox Populism: Branding Conservatism as Working Class*. Cambridge: Cambridge University Press.

Peck, R. (2014). 'You say rich, I say job creator': How Fox News framed the Great Recession through the moral discourse of producerism. *Media, Culture & Society,* 36(4), 526–535.

Schubert, C. (2021). Multimodal cohesion in persuasive discourse. *Discourse, Context & Media*, 43, 1–10.

Tumber, H. & Waisbord, S. (2021). Media, disinformation, and populism: Problems and responses. In H. Tumber & S. Waisbord (Eds.), *The Routledge Companion to Media Disinformation and Populism* (pp. 13–26). London-New York: Routledge.

Watkins, S.C. (2019). *Don't Knock the Hustle*. Boston: Beacon Press.

Wells, C. & Rochefort, A. (2021). Populism and misinformation from the American Revolution to the Twenty-First-Century United States. In H. Tumber & S. Waisbord (Eds.), *The Routledge Companion to Media Disinformation and Populism* (pp. 345–355). London-New York: Routledge.

3 The discursive construction, delegitimization, and defense of political identities

Introduction

In her preface to *The Routledge Handbook of Language and Identity,* published in 2016, Bonny Norton affirms:

> language is not only a linguistic system of signs and symbols, but also a complex social practice in which the value and meaning of a given utterance – whether oral or written – is partly determined by the value ascribed to a particular speaker or writer. This value, in turn, is best understood with reference to complex social and cultural practices, and negotiated in the context of shifting relations of power.
>
> (p. xxii)

The present chapter provides a conceptual framework for the three primary angles used to approach the discursive construction of Alexandria Ocasio-Cortez's political self in this book. To frame the study of Ocasio-Cortez's presentation of her identity during her first primary campaign (Chapter 4), it begins by describing facets that have been deemed pivotal in the construction of a candidate's political identity – "the composite image the candidate so delicately crafted amid the constant churn of the political campaign" (Parry-Giles & Steudeman, 2017, p. 82) – or narrative, existential and historical coherence, and positioning theory. Next, it describes how delegitimization, recontextualization, and re-entextualization are understood in this book, and particularly within the discussion of how opposition media addressed Ocasio-Cortez (Chapter 5). The chapter concludes with a review of stance, which is the primary lens through which the defense of Ocasio-Cortez's identity is analyzed in Chapter 6.

DOI: 10.4324/9781003273103-3

Constructing (political) selves: positioning, narrative, and coherence

Parry-Giles and Steudeman (2017) argue that "campaigns and elections are mostly (if not exclusively) about candidates rather than issues" (p. 67), such that voters' opinions of different facets of candidates' political identities – like their authenticity, credibility, and likeability – determine their stances on policy. Identity construction is, therefore, paramount for successful political outcomes.

The present work adopts the perspective that identity construction – within and outside the political realm – is a process best explored using the notion of "identity work," or "the range of activities individuals engage in to create, present, and sustain personal identities that are congruent with and supportive of the self-concept" (Snow & Anderson, 1987, p. 1348). Processes of identity formation involve the performance of identities in the attempt to gain recognition and acceptance as a certain "kind of person" (Gee, 2015, p. 3). People employ many strategies to achieve these ends, such as appealing to "emblematic resources," or characterizing features of identities that people point to when speaking of or performing within a given identity category (Blommaert & Varis, 2011, p. 4). As suggested in the introduction to this chapter, this book also takes a discursive approach to the study of identity construction, which regards identities "as constituted through situated practices of language use" (Brown, 2019, p. 9). Identity construction is neither context-free nor intramental. It relies on dialogical relations with others.

One way in which the dialogic process of identity construction has been unpacked is with positioning theory. Davies and Harré (1990) define positioning as "the discursive process whereby selves are located in conversations as observably and subjectively coherent participants in jointly produced story lines" (p. 48). In interactions, participants simultaneously position the other while positioning themselves, and they shift positions, at times even contradictorily, during discourse resulting in the creation of various "possible selves" (Harré & van Langenhove, 1991). This approach to identity construction casts identities as ephemeral positions that "involve shifts in power, access, or blocking of access, to certain features of claimed or desired identity" (Davies & Harré, 1990, p. 49).

Positioning theory has become an important tool in the analysis of discourse and interaction. Sclafani (2018) presented an illuminating example of the effectiveness of interactional sociolinguistic approaches including positioning theory in the study of political discourse as identity performance, arguing in favor of applying this theory to the analysis of political actors because they enact performances in the attempt to both "actively position themselves as a certain type of person" and to respond to "the way they have been positioned by others" (p. 405). Sclafani (2018) presents a three-tiered analysis of a campaign advertisement of a female candidate to the US Senate. Delving into the story told, the narration by a male third party, and the way it reinforces existing party narratives, the analysis displays how the advertisement accomplished the construction of the candidate's political self as a strong, conservative, female leader.

Bucholtz and Hall (2005) drew on positioning theory to develop the relationality principle which defines the process of identity construction as "intersubjective relations of sameness and difference, realness and fakeness, power and disempowerment" (p. 608). They formulated three sets of tactics, termed the tactics of intersubjectivity, to serve as tools to explain how individuals dialogically establish and then shift their own and others' positioning in intersubjective relations. The first set, *adequation* and *distinction*, captures processes related to the erasure of discordant elements or the accentuation of differences. The second set of tactics, *authentication* and *denaturalization*, concerns processes related to claims for "real" identities or the signaling of imposture. The third set is *authorization* and *illegitimation*, which involves the processes by which particular social identities and the power structures that sanction identities are legitimated, while others are suppressed and become non-choices (Bucholtz & Hall, 2004).

The relational and dialogic nature of identity construction implies that the legitimacy of (inhabited) identities can be questioned, challenged, or altogether refuted. A person "has to 'have' enough of the emblematic features in order to be ratified as an authentic member of an identity category" (Blommaert & Varis, 2011, p. 4). Access to and fluency in these constantly changing emblems is not evenly allocated, so authenticity can be seen as a privilege reserved for a select few. Yet, authenticity is essential in many domains and, as suggested earlier, the desire to be recognized and ratified as authentic and credible is a primary concern for politicians.

Chilton (2004) has argued that "political discourse involves, among other things, the promotion of representations," and he explains that:

> a pervasive feature of representation is the evident need for political speakers to imbue their utterances with evidence,

authority and truth, a process that we shall refer to in broad terms, in the context of political discourse, as 'legitimisation' [...] Political speakers have to guard against the operation of their audience's 'cheater detectors' and provide guarantees for the truth of their sayings.

(p. 23)

Processes of legitimization, which will be the focus of the next section of this chapter, are, therefore, pivotal for politicians to present themselves as credible and authoritative and preempt challenges to their constructed selves. These efforts should weave together a narrative designed to build, advance, and disseminate political identities. In fact, the successful construction of political identities can be understood as the development of coherent narratives, an especially potent means of persuasion (Braddock & Dillard, 2016).

Lejano and Nero (2020), whose *The Power of Narrative* is dedicated to describing the narrative of climate skepticism and how it functions and spreads, helpfully define narrative as:

the form by which people emplot different aspects, events, and characters (e.g., related to climate science) and make everything connect into a meaningful whole (i.e., a plot). Narrative takes the otherwise inchoate things, events, and places in a novel (or a life) and makes everything fit together.

(p. 8)

Narratives need not be constructed in formal, traditional means. Lejano and Nero (2020) specify that even tweets can constitute narrative "if one or more tweets describe a logical set of ideas or sequence of events that constitute a coherent chain" (p. 8). Since Twitter holds an increasingly important role in today's political communication, as already elaborated in Chapter 2, the role of this social media platform in crafting a narrative can provide novel insights into how political identities are constructed.

The narratives created by and about political candidates have long been studied by analysts of political discourse. One particularly fruitful area of study relevant for the present work has concerned coherence. Candidates carefully communicate their experiences, achievements, and future projections well aware that their statements are closely monitored (by potential voters, their opponents, and the media) for potential inaccuracies and inconsistencies, which, if revealed, may result in the charge that a candidate lied or betrayed a promise and may, therefore, jeopardize his or her race. To preempt these attacks, candidates aim to present and perpetuate a noncontradictory image of themselves by means of developing what Duranti (2006) called existential coherence, or "a coherence of actions, thoughts, and words aimed as supporting a PERSON in the anthropological sense of a culturally identifiable type of social being" (p. 472). Duranti's (2006) analysis of the campaign speeches and debates of a US Congressional candidate revealed three discursive strategies used in the construction of existential coherence. The first strategy, or narratives of belonging, involves the linear presentation of life events to demonstrate a candidate's emotional and moral connection to the district; the second involves making the present a "natural extension" of the candidate's past experience(s); and the third involves raising attention to potential contradictions to show that they are not contradictions. These strategies help candidates justify their decisions, not least deciding to run for office, and "to construct the kind of person that they want the voters to know and believe in" (p. 492).

Meade and Robles (2017) built on Duranti's (2006) work to introduce the concept of historical coherence, which "links the candidate directly with particular versions of history to show that the candidate's words and actions are congruent with those of popular or well-known historical, archetypal, or stereotypical figures" (p. 407), in their examination of multimodal strategies used in American political ads. Three historical coherence-building strategies emerged including the use of narratives that position the candidate alongside renowned historical figures, the preemption of accusations of noncoherence, and the candidate's portrayal as a champion of freedom. Multimodal techniques that draw on historical language, images, and figures make it possible for candidates to emplot themselves seamlessly within larger historical narratives.

Of course, while narratives can be helpful and powerful tools for the construction of political identities, narratives can also be constructed with the aim of calling into question and even dismantling carefully crafted identities. The following section examines this phenomenon more closely.

Contesting the opposition: delegitimization and recontextualization

Rojo and van Dijk (1997) maintain that "political power and legitimacy are permanently at risk" (p. 524). Those in power face incessant challenges from many fronts – including political opponents, mass media, alternative media, and even the public, who in the post-digital era have the potential to amass a large audience – to their legitimacy. Successful delegitimization generally undermines the actions, policies, or words of an actor or group, and its effects can subvert the actor, their position, and their leadership as well. While legitimization is "the creation of a sense of positive, beneficial, ethical, understandable, necessary or otherwise acceptable action in a specific setting," delegitimization involves "establishing a sense of negative, morally reprehensible or otherwise unacceptable action or overall state of affairs" (Vaara, 2014, p. 503). The self-legitimization of political actors and other-delegitimization of foes is about "claiming authority and depriving the political opponent of this authority" (Neag & Berger, 2019, p. 216). Thus, it can be viewed as a form of positive self- and negative other-presentation.

Processes of (de)legitimization occur almost exclusively discursively. Hence, an understanding of these processes requires consideration of its linguistic, communicative, and interactional elements (Rojo & van Dijk, 1997). It follows, therefore, that one of the most prolific veins of research into legitimization has employed (critical) discourse analysis. Most of this research has applied Theo van Leeuwen's (2007, 2008) categories for the critical analysis of the construction of (de)legitimization in discourse. van Leeuwen (2008, p. 105–106) defines these four legitimization categories as follows:

1 Authorization: reference to the authority of tradition, custom, law, and/or persons in whom institutional authority of some kind is vested.
2 Moral evaluation: (often very oblique) reference to value systems.
3 Rationalization: reference to the goals and uses of institutionalized social action and the knowledges that society has constructed to endow them with cognitive validity.
4 Mythopoesis: conveyed through narratives whose outcomes reward legitimate actions and punish nonlegitimate actions.

The use of these categories in the analysis of discursive legitimization strategies has provided fruitful insights into the discursive construction of (de)legitimization by myriad institutions and actors across domains. For instance, Vaara (2014) uncovered how, within a crisis of institutional (Eurozone) legitimacy, evidence of all four categories were used in Finnish media texts, including both position- and knowledge-based authorization, rationalizations centered on economic arguments, moral evaluations based on unfairness, and mythopoesis involving alternative future scenarios.

The multimodal dimension of (de)legitimization has become an increasingly popular object of research. Roughly 15 years ago, van Leeuwen (2008) described how visuals and music can function to (de)legitimize social practices, and more recent research has studied this phenomenon in light of a wider array of affordances provided by new media. In his CDA study of Obama's political ads in the 2008 US presidential campaign, Mackay (2013) displays the significance of multimodality to legitimization: visual and auditory elements served to legitimize the then-candidate by emphasizing certain features of a recontextualized speech, and by positioning him and his voters as cutting-edge and clever. Ross and Rivers (2017) use multimodal discourse analysis to examine how Internet memes were employed to "criticize, deride, and mock" the 2016 US presidential candidates (p. 1). The user-generated Internet memes they examine present an important departure from most studies that have analyzed (de)legitimization in formal, non-multimodal texts. Ross and Rivers (2017) both unveiled how van Leeuwen's (2008) (de)legitimization categories were used by meme creators and found that these users engaged in acts of political participation by undermining their opponents' political campaign.

Neag and Berger (2019) present a particularly interesting study of (de)legitimization in political discourse on social media with a focus on the campaign of self-defined "joke" party Hungarian Two-tailed Dog Party (HTDP), which turned parody into political acts as they subverted dominant Hungarian governmental campaigns through humor. The authors analyzed the delegitimization of the ruling coalition enacted in selected posts on the Facebook account of the HTDP by means of a readaptation of the five legitimization strategies in political discourse articulated in Reyes (2011). The original categories – legitimization through emotions, a hypothetical future, rationality, voices of expertise, and altruism – became delegitimization through comic relief, a ridiculed hypothetical future, irrationality, voice of the nonexperts, and ridiculed altruism. In describing these delegitimization processes, Neag and Berger (2019) provide tools for the analysis of delegitimization through parody, an increasingly important means used in the challenge of political identities. Furthermore, they display the importance of taking heed of user-generated online communication and social media as spaces of (de)legitimization in which dominant voices are (de)privileged and political discourse is actively shaped. One of the mechanisms that have come to the fore in the study of delegitimization is the movement of texts and discourses across contexts. Anthropologists Richard Bauman and Charles L. Briggs (1990) argued in favor of more process-oriented understandings – over object-centered notions – of context and text. While the focus of their article was performance-based studies, their analysis shed some early insights into how discourse is negotiated, assessed, valued, and transformed that are applicable beyond this domain. Their discussion of entextualization – "the process of rendering discourse extractable, of making a stretch of linguistic production into a unit – a *text* – that can be lifted out of its interactional setting" (Bauman & Briggs, 1990, p. 73) – was particularly useful to this end. Discourse becomes decontextualized when it is detached from its situational context, and it is recontextualized into another context. This is a transformational process: the recontextualized text carries aspects from its earlier context and, as it is recentered, it gains new forms, functions, and meanings. Importantly, this process hinges on power. Bauman and Briggs (1990) explained that to decontextualize and recontextualize a text is "an act of control" due to "differential access to texts, differential legitimacy in claims to and use of texts, differential competence in the use of texts, and differential values attaching to various types of texts" (p. 76).

Sociolinguists and discourse analysts have since applied these concepts widely. Much work has been done on recontextualization within CDA studies, spearheaded by Ruth Wodak, Norman Fairclough, and Theo van Leeuwen. Indeed, in their coauthored work, Wodak and Fairclough (2010) argue that recontextualization can be productively used as a salient CDA category. They maintain that recontextualization – "whereby texts (and the discourses and genres which they deploy) move between spatially and temporally different contexts, and are subject to transformations whose nature depends upon relationships and differences between such contexts" (p. 22) – is concretely manifested in the intertextuality and interdiscursivity of texts. To explain how elements of social events are selectively "filtered" in representations across contexts, Fairclough (2003, p. 139) expanded an existing framework to develop the following "recontextualizing principles," which are used as an interpretative key in Chapter 5 of the present book: the exclusion/inclusion and foregrounding/backgrounding of elements (presence); the degree of abstraction/generalization (abstraction); the order of representation (arrangement); and additions in representing events including explanations, legitimizations and evaluations (additions). Re-entextualization has been used less frequently but not less productively in the literature. As already stated in Chapter 2, Blommaert (2020) theorized that today complex structures of communication convey political discourse, and this often occurs via processes of re-entextualization. For Blommaert (2020), entextualization refers to

> the process by means of which discourses are successively or simultaneously decontextualized and metadiscursively recontextualized, so that they become a new discourse associated to a new context and accompanied by a particular metadiscourse which provides a sort of 'preferred reading' for the discourse.
> (p. 398)

Online "copy" processes such as reposts and retweets do not constitute a series of repetitions of "the same" message but a series of re-entextualizations of a transformed message (Blommaert, 2020). In the realm of political discourse, the development of user-generated online content – whether a simple retweet, meme, or comment – involves a user's appropriation of a politician's message and its insertion into "an entirely new act of communication involving a new producer (the user) and addressees (the user's own network of online 'friends' or 'followers') in a new kind of interaction" with characteristics that "diverge strongly from those of the original ('input') act" (Blommaert, 2020, p. 399).

Once, the coverage and interpretation of political talk was reserved for the press's exclusive community. The online realm has afforded the opportunity for anyone to obtain access to and engage directly with political discourse, reframing and rekeying it for new purposes and for new audiences. Since one of the intended effects of the transformations inherent in recontextualization and re-entextualization of political discourse may, in fact, be the delegitimization of political actors, this means that even anonymous users can take on this powerful act.

The delegitimization of political rivals can originate from many different actors (e.g., online users or elected officials), can take on many forms (e.g., formal speeches or memes), and can have various aims (e.g., undermining politicians' authenticity, credibility, or coherence). Acts of legitimization, therefore, become crucial to defend the constructed political identities and to reclaim approval.

The discussion of the construction and delegitimization of political identities thus far has acknowledged but not stressed the dialogical and intersubjective dimensions of these various facets of political discourse. The next section, however, shifts emphasis to the defense of political identities against delegitimating attacks through the lens of stance-taking, which, therefore, foregrounds these dimensions.

Taking a stance in the defense of identities

The final angle considered in this book is the defense and consolidation of political identities. The pursuit of the examination of this phenomenon involves regard of aspects that have been described previously in this chapter. Challenges to politician's credibility and authenticity, for instance, can involve repair work aimed at reinforcing the coherence of personal narratives as well as efforts to achieve self-legitimization and the delegitimization of the source of the attack. At its core, the safeguarding of political selves in response to criticism is relational and dialogic. Thus, the primary perspective that is taken for the analysis of this phenomenon is stance, which functions as a mediator between interaction and identity (Woodhams, 2019).

According to Du Bois (2007), stance is "a public act by a social actor, achieved dialogically through overt communicative means, of simultaneously evaluating objects, positioning subjects (self and others), and aligning with other subjects, with respect to any salient dimension of the sociocultural field" (p. 163). Stances, which rely on the context of the utterance (Kiesling et al., 2018), encode speakers' attitudes toward the stance object, their moods, evaluations, points of view, and opinions at different levels of language including lexis, grammar, style, and pragmatics (Ushchyna, 2014). Kiesling (2011) has theorized that stance is at the core of what drives people to employ particular discourses, sociolinguistic variables, or lexical items since it underpins the type of person that users wish to project with talk, and (groups of) language users tend to prefer certain stances such that "the language forms used to create this stance becomes associated, or indexed, with some aspect of the speaker's identity or the speech event" (p. 1).

Further insights in this light can be gleaned by investigations into style, which have unearthed the relationship(s) between identity and stance. Style has been retheorized "as a multimodal and multidimensional cluster of linguistic and other semiotic practices for the display of identities in interaction" (Bucholtz, 2009, p. 146). A burgeoning strand of research has applied indexicality to the exploration of stylistic practice to unearth the ideologically bound and fleeting interactional moves through which social actors take stances, create (dis)alignments, and construct personas. Indexical processes may construct identity within interaction directly, where linguistic forms index interactional stances, or indirectly, where ideological associations emerge between these linguistic forms and social types (for instance, some forms come to be seen as inherently feminine or masculine).

Recent studies have begun to unearth how stances are enacted in online contexts. Wang (2020) combines stancetaking and frame theory to analyze participant interactions and different types of alignment – defined as synonymous with Goffman's (1981) notion of footing – in Facebook comments regarding Taiwan's same-sex marriage legislation. Wang (2020) finds that a focus on language affords insights into the mediated performance involved in the production and negotiation of information on social media, of which alignment is the central mechanism. Kiesling et al. (2018) put forth a novel computational operationalization of interpersonal stancetaking in the study of conversational threads from Reddit. The researchers investigate the thread structure and linguistic properties of stancetaking by undertaking a close analysis of the stance focus – or "the thing that is made most relevant by an utterance" (p. 688) based on Du Bois' (2007) stance object – and three linked stance dimensions: affect – "the polarity or quality of the stance to the stance focus" –, investment – "how strongly invested in the talk the speaker is" –, and alignment – "how much a speaker/writer aligns (or not) to their interlocutor(s), real or imagined" (p. 688). Kiesling et al. (2018) exhibit evidence that dividing stance into these three dimensions fosters a more productive analysis of the relational aspects and meanings of interaction.

A strand of this recent research has shed light onto the role of stances in the identity construction and consolidation of public figures. For instance, Valentinsson (2018) uncovers the stance-taking moves that American celebrity Lady Gaga deploys to fashion an authentic celebrity persona, usefully analyzing two different data sources: tweets and interviews. On the one hand, her tweets suggest the celebrity's effort to create a stance of alignment with her fans (above all other audiences) by citing intimate relationships with them, using inclusive plural pronouns, and directly responding to fans. On the other hand, interviews reveal the construction of stances of disalignment with the media by flouting the norms of celebrity interviews and using strategies such as critique, dismissal, and reframing of journalist questions. Usher (2016) instead offers an analysis of the Twitter and Facebook profiles of the political leaders running in the 2015 UK "short campaign" to examine how they constructed their political personas on social network sites. Usher (2016) notes that "political public persona on [social network sites] straddles lines between authority as public figures and authenticity as users" (p. 23). While the electoral successes of Conservatives suggest that their highly professionalized and resourced use of social network sites is a winning strategy, Nigel Farage's "digital dog-whistling" garnered him the greatest increase in likes during the campaign and succeeded at attracting attention and increasing visibility of himself and his party (p. 38).

In the face of attack and criticism, modern politicians employ a host of tools at their disposal to defend their political identities and standpoints and to reclaim approval and legitimacy. New media have altered the ways in which these types of responses are structured, conveyed, and received. They have influenced how style and stance are enacted by contemporary political actors and have afforded the opportunity for scholars to analyze this enactment, as it is rendered more explicit by the direct line between politicians and the public that the hybrid media system provides. They also grant the possibility to trace the differences and similarities in how stancetaking occurs in different settings with different audiences, resources, and levels of formality.

This chapter began with Norton's (2016) definition of language as a social practice whose value is contingent on the power of its users. The role of power in language is unequivocal in political discourse where political actors constantly seek legitimization, approval, and endorsement from their constituents, other politicians, the press, and the public at large. The overarching concepts discussed in this chapter guide the analysis of the linguistic and communicative processes by which a particular language user – in this case a political actor – endeavored to forge, strengthen, and defend a valuable political identity. Specifically, the next three chapters examine how Alexandria Ocasio-Cortez discursively built her political persona and negotiated her constructed identity, how she was challenged and attacked by the opposition, and how she safeguarded her political identity and fought, discursively, to emerge triumphant.

References

Bauman, R. & Briggs, C.L. (1990). Poetics and performances as critical perspectives on language and social life. *Annual Review of Anthropology,* 19, 59–88.

Blommaert, J. (2020). Political discourse in post-digital societies. *Trabalhos em Linguística Aplicada,* 59(1), 390–403.

Blommaert, J. & Varis, P. (2011). Enough is enough: The heuristics of authenticity in superdiversity. *Working Papers in Urban Language & Literacies,* 76, 1–13.

Braddock, K. & Dillard, J. P. (2016). Meta-analytic evidence for the persuasive effect of narratives on beliefs, attitudes, intentions, and behaviors. *Communication Monographs,* 83(4), 446–467.

Brown, A.D. (2019). Identities in organization studies. *Organization Studies,* 40(1), 7–22.

Bucholtz, M. (2009). From stance to style: Gender, interaction, and indexicality in Mexican immigrant youth slang. In A. Jaffe (Ed.), *Stance: Sociolinguistic Perspectives* (pp. 146–170). Oxford: Oxford University Press.

Bucholtz, M. & Hall, K. (2005). Identity and interaction: A sociocultural linguistic approach. *Discourse Studies,* 7(4–5), 585–614.

Bucholtz, M. & Hall, K. (2004). Language and identity. In A. Duranti (Ed.), *A Companion to Linguistic Anthropology* (pp. 369–394). Oxford: Blackwell.

Chilton, P. (2004). *Analysing Political Discourse.* London-New York: Routledge.

Davies, B. & Harré, R. (1990). Positioning: The discursive production of Selves. *Journal for the Theory of Social Behaviour,* 20(1), 43–63.

Du Bois, J.W. (2007). The stance triangle. In R. Englebretson (Ed.), *Stancetaking in Discourse: Subjectivity, Evaluation, Interaction* (pp. 139–182). Amsterdam/Philadelphia: John Benjamins.

Duranti, A. (2006). Narrating the political self in a campaign for U.S. Congress. *Language in Society,* 35(4), 467–497.

Fairclough, N. (2003). *Analyzing Discourse: Textual Analysis for Social Research.* London: Routledge.

Gee, J.P. (2015). *Social Linguistics and Literacies: Ideology in Discourses* (5th ed.). New York: Routledge.

Goffman, E. (1981). *Forms of Talk.* Philadelphia: University of Pennsylvania Press.

Harré, R. & van Langenhove, L. (1991). Varieties of positionings. *Journal for the Theory of Social Behaviour,* 21(4), 393–407.

Kiesling, S. (2011). Stance in context: Affect, alignment and investment in the analysis of stancetaking. Paper presented at *iMean conference,* 15 April 2011, The University of the West of England, Bristol, UK.

Kiesling, S.F., et al. (2018). Interactional stancetaking in online forums. *Computational Linguistics,* 44(4), 683–718.

Lejano, R.P. & Nero, S. (2020). *The Power of Narrative: Climate Skepticism and the Deconstruction of Science*. New York: Oxford University Press.

Mackay, R.R. (2013). Multimodal legitimation: Looking at and listening to Obama's ads. In P. Cap & U. Okulska (Eds.), *Analyzing Genres in Political Communication: Theory and Practice* (pp. 345–377). Amsterdam-Philadelphia: John Benjamins.

Meade, M. & Robles, J. (2017). Historical and existential coherence in political commercials. *Discourse & Communication*, 11(4), 404–432.

Neag, A. & Berger, R. (2019). Always on, but never there? Political parody, the Carnivalesque and the rise of the 'Nectorate'. In A.S. Ross & D.J. Rivers (Eds.), *Discourses of (De)Legitimization* (pp. 211–227). New York-London: Routledge.

Norton, B. (2016). Preface. In S. Preece (Ed.), *The Routledge Handbook of Language and Identity* (pp. xxii–xxiv). New York: Routledge.

Parry-Giles, T. & Steudeman, M.J. (2017). Crafting character, moving history: John McCain's political identity in the 2008 presidential campaign. *Quarterly Journal of Speech*, 103(1–2), 66–89.

Reyes, A. (2011). Strategies of legitimization in political discourse: From words to actions. *Discourse & Society*, 22(6), 781–807.

Rojo, L.M. & van Dijk, T.A. (1997). "There was a problem, and it was solved!": Legitimating the expulsion of 'Illegal' migrants in Spanish parliamentary discourse. *Discourse & Society*, 8(4), 523–566.

Ross, A.S. & Rivers, D.J. (2017). Digital cultures of political participation. *Discourse, Context and Media*, 16, 1–11.

Sclafani, J. (2018). Performing politics. In R. Wodak & B. Forchtner (Eds.), *The Routledge Handbook of Language and Politics* (pp. 398–411). Oxon-New York: Routledge.

Snow, D.A. & Anderson, L. (1987). Identity work among the homeless: The verbal construction and avowal of personal identities. *American Journal of Sociology*, 92, 1336–1371.

Ushchyna, V. (2014). Stancetaking in the discourse on risk identities construed. In M. Thormählen &C. Paradis (Eds.), *Subjectivity and Epistemicity: Corpus, Discourse, and Literary Approaches to Stance* (pp. 215–238). Lund: Lund University Press.

Usher, B. (2016). ME, YOU, and US: Constructing political persona on social networks during the 2015 UK general election. *Persona Studies*, 2(2), 19–41.

Vaara, E. (2014). Struggles over legitimacy in the Eurozone crisis: Discursive legitimation strategies and their ideological underpinnings. *Discourse & Society*, 25(4), 500–518.

Valentinsson, M-C. (2018). Stance and the construction of authentic celebrity persona. *Language in Society*, 47, 715–740.

van Leeuwen, T. (2008). *Discourse and Practice*. Oxford: Oxford University Press.

van Leeuwen, T. (2007). Legitimation in Discourse and Communication, *Discourse & Communication,* 1(1), 91–112.

Wang, P.-H. (2020). Stance, framing, and the construction of reality in Facebook comments about Taiwan's same-sex marriage bills. *Discourse & Society,* 31(2), 218–234.

Wodak, R. & Fairclough, N. (2010). Recontextualizing European higher education policies: The cases of Austria and Romania. *Critical Discourse Studies,* 7(1), 19–40.

Woodhams, J.M. (2019). *Political Identity in Discourse.* Cham: Palgrave Macmillan.

4 "It's time for one of us"

The construction of Alexandria Ocasio-Cortez's political self during her first campaign

Introduction

Alexandria Ocasio-Cortez is currently one of the most recognizable US Representatives – and, I would argue, US politicians – worldwide. However, when she embarked on her campaign for the 2018 Democratic primary race for the US House of Representatives of New York's 14th District (NY-14) just five years ago, for most, Ocasio-Cortez was an unknown newcomer to the political scene. The need to create a narrative that rationalized her candidacy was pressing to forestall attacks and to preempt the charge that she was too unconventional, too young, and too inexperienced to compete and eventually claim this post.

If, as argued in Chapter 3, political candidates strive to craft a coherent sense of "who they are" for their constituents and the wider public (Parry-Giles & Steudeman, 2017), how is this achieved by a first-time candidate chosen and backed specifically because she had little to no political experience? This chapter examines how Ocasio-Cortez discursively constructed a political identity designed to project a vision that she was at once one of "the people" and different from "the elite" but still competent and electable. It applies corpus analytical and interactional sociolinguistic approaches to study the strategies, mechanisms, and features within selected content that she created, produced, and shared during her first campaign. Specifically, it examines her narration of the character, plot, and setting within her campaign advertisement and her tweets, already introduced in Chapter 2, that presented and defined her political identity.

This chapter opens with a brief overview of the selected content and the analytical methods employed. It then proceeds with a close look at the visual and textual elements of Ocasio-Cortez's viral campaign video before providing a detailed description of the findings of the analysis of her tweets by disclosing the linguistic and non-textual features that the Representative used to construct belonging and to authenticate different facets of her identity. To see the distinguishing features of Ocasio-Cortez's Twitter use, a comparative analysis of her tweets to those of other Representatives follows. The chapter closes with a summary of the narrative Ocasio-Cortez crafted of herself as an ordinary American, a left-wing populist, and a trailblazer during her first political campaign.

The selected viral content of Ocasio-Cortez's first campaign

While campaign ads have been a staple of political advertising within campaigns, with the first prototype airing in an American movie theater close to a century ago (Mackay, 2013), Twitter constitutes a relatively new genre that compels all users – and candidates – to adapt to its limitations (initially 140 and later 280 characters) and its unique conventions (e.g., re-tweeting, hashtags, and mentions). Notwithstanding their stylistic and historical differences, both genres play an important part in today's political campaigns. In addition, and relevant for the present chapter, they both attracted viral attention and served as platforms through which Ocasio-Cortez stood out from other candidates.

The Courage to Change campaign video

Ocasio-Cortez's two-minute campaign advertisement *The Courage to Change*, for which the candidate wrote the script and delivered the voice-over, was released in May 2018, just a month before the primary election. It generated more than 300,000 online views in the first day alone and became the most-watched political campaign video of the season (Watkins, 2019). Even though campaign ads have a well-established tradition in the promotion of candidates (see Chapter 2), the novelty of the form of Ocasio-Cortez's campaign ad as well as the attention it garnered render this content worthy of investigation as a unique vehicle through which the candidate constructed her political self.

Several steps were taken in the analysis of *The Courage to Change*. In line with the methodology employed in the multimodal analysis of campaign videos described in Schubert (2021), the transcription and subsequent analysis focused on three semiotic layers. The spoken words, written text, and visual images of the advertisement were manually transcribed into a table of which an excerpt is provided as an Appendix at the end of this book. These multiple layers aimed to increase sensitivity to semiotic and embodied resources, and to take heed of the intentionality of commercial creators who use these resources to construct, complement, and/or emphasize what is said (Meade & Robles, 2017).

@AOC tweets and corpus analysis

The tweets analyzed in this chapter were those posted by Ocasio-Cortez (using the Twitter handle @AOC) during a roughly 18-month period that began on 17 May 2017, when she officially announced her candidacy on Twitter, and ended before polls closed on 6 November 2018, the day of the Congressional election. The resulting 3,968 Tweets (excluding retweets) amounted to a 121,738-token corpus (named "AOC first campaign"). The corpus was analyzed using Sketch Engine, an online text analysis tool (https://www.sketchengine.eu/, Kilgarriff et al., 2014), to explore the most frequently used words and symbols, concordance results, and the grammatical and collocational behaviors of selected words. Comparative keyword analysis was also performed against a reference corpus constituted by original tweets posted by US Representatives of the 116th Congress, developed from a larger corpus created by Wrubel and Kerchner (2020), named "Reference." This reference corpus was deemed fitting because it consisted of tweets posted by US politicians in the same period, referred to the same context, and used the same variety of English (US English). The result of this comparative analysis, for which Sketch Engine uses statistical tests based on the simple maths method (Kilgarriff, 2009), is the identification of a list of keywords, or words that occur "with unusual frequency in a given text" (Scott, 1997, p. 236). The purpose of this first level of analysis was to obtain a nuanced understanding of the linguistic resources that the candidate employed in the construction of her political self.

A summary of the corpora follows:

- AOC first campaign: Original @AOC tweets from May 2017 to November 2018 – 3,968 tweets (121,738 tokens)
- Reference: Original tweets from 75 randomly selected US Representatives of the 116th Congress from May 2017 to November 2018 – 35,165 tweets (1,022,146 tokens)

Common analytical approach

In addition to the approaches described above, to explore the linguistic and semiotic resources and strategies utilized by the candidate in the construction of her political self and in her attempt to preserve coherence in her campaign video and tweets, following Sclafani (2018), an interactional sociolinguistics lens was applied to the analysis of discourse, which considers both frames and positioning. Frames supply a structure on which people rely to produce and interpret meaning: they guide expectations during talk and shape understandings of preceding talk. Frames can be examined as multiple and negotiable interpretive universes and interactional achievements within which interlocutors can shift footing (Sclafani, 2018). Positioning theory allows us to consider that candidates may construct themselves and others at different levels including within the stories they tell; may challenge contradictory narratives and positioning done to them; and may position themselves with respect to larger (national or historical) storylines. To perform this multileveled analysis, this study utilizes Bucholtz and Halls' (2005) tactics of intersubjectivity framework, discussed in Chapter 3, which includes the following sets of tactics: *adequation* and *distinction*; *authentication* and *denaturalization*; and *authorization* and *illegitimation*. These tactics serve as tools to investigate how political candidates dialogically establish and shift their own and others' positioning. They contribute to the study by considering the larger social and political structures within which interactions exist (and the constraints that these may yield), and the discursive construction and negotiation of the multiple facets of the candidate's identity.

The construction of a coherent political self in *The Courage to Change*

The two-minute campaign advertisement *The Courage to Change* begins with the affirmation: "Women like me aren't supposed to run for office," which establishes an exclusionary frame. By choosing to state "women like me" and not "people like me," Ocasio-Cortez explicitly foregrounds gender. As she pronounces these words, the accompanying image, which is shown on the left in Figure 4.1, adds an interpretative key for what "women like me" might imply: Ocasio-Cortez, a young woman of color, is shown alone in her Bronx apartment tying up her hair. The absence of aides or volunteers projects an image of the candidate as independent and self-sufficient. The

Figure 4.1 Screenshots from The Courage to Change.

mundane act performed in an unostentatious setting suggests to the viewer that Ocasio-Cortez lacks a curated – and arguably crafted – image. She presents herself as genuine and simple, as authentic. Moreover, her image is not central in the frame and her reflection in the mirror is partial and fleeting. With this video-style technique, an aspect of *adequation* – or the downplaying of "differences irrelevant or damaging to ongoing efforts to adequate two people or groups" (Bucholtz & Hall, 2005, p. 599) – is realized: the viewer may surmise that it is Ocasio-Cortez, but the woman in the shot could ostensibly be any woman performing the familiar task.

After the first affirmation of the video, Ocasio-Cortez widens the scope and describes herself in terms of her birthplace, her family's socioeconomic status, and her parents' birthplaces (lines 2–4 in the Appendix) while she is shown doing things that any New Yorker might do (e.g., walking to the subway, taking public transportation). She even slips into her heels on a subway platform (Figure 4.1, right). The visual content – and to a lesser extent, the verbal content – foregrounds the "similarities viewed as salient to and supportive of the immediate project of identity work" (Bucholtz & Hall, 2005, p. 599), or the similarities between the candidate and her NYC constituents. Ocasio-Cortez then lists her employment experience, detailing her community-based work, service sector jobs, and working-class status, but she fails to mention either her policy and political campaign experience or her relevant college major. She instead specifies: "going into politics wasn't in the plan" (line 8). The candidate is, thus, framed – both verbally and visually; both by what is stated and what is omitted – as an ordinary person and member of the NY-14 community.

In stating that women of her class, ethnicity, or birthplace are not "supposed to run for office" and that running for office "wasn't in the plan," Ocasio-Cortez can achieve two aims. On the one hand, she can anticipate and preempt viewers' potential skepticism of her

The construction of Alexandria Ocasio-Cortez's political self 43

candidacy on the grounds that she is inexperienced by explicitly acknowledging these potential contradictions through oppositional language and syntactic negation. On the other hand, she can place the perceived lack of coherence at the heart of the matter: the fact that she is not a typical candidate – particularly in her district – is itself the problematic issue and can be drawn on as a resource to decry social justice abuses against her community.

Inequity and injustice underpin and lay bare a primary reason Ocasio-Cortez provides for running for office: the system that denies representation must change. By running for office (therefore, pursuing something that she is not "supposed to" do), Ocasio-Cortez positions herself as an antiestablishment candidate[1] not only because of her Democratic Socialist platform, which she describes later in the video, but because of her class, gender, ethnicity, and birthplace. Ocasio-Cortez, thus, frames herself not as an individual vying for political office but as someone for whom political participation has been suppressed and not sanctioned. Through this lens, Ocasio-Cortez's primary race can be interpreted synecdochically as the plight of "the people" who, like her, have been denied political participation and representation. Ocasio-Cortez's run for office *authenticates* her identity and situates her in congruence with historical social justice and civil rights figures (Bucholtz & Hall, 2005). Like those who preceded her, as emblematized by the title of the video, the candidate exhibits courage in facing this enterprise. Indeed, the only instance in which the candidate speaks directly to the camera (and to her viewers) is to utter: "It takes political courage."

The construction of Ocasio-Cortez's political self is achieved just as much by stating what she is as by stating what she is not. In fact, Ocasio-Cortez's narrative work that positions her as a representative, working-class person is reinforced in the video by framing her opponent as a profiteer with limited ties to the community, as follows:

> a Democrat who takes corporate money, profits off foreclosure, doesn't live here, doesn't send his kids to our schools, doesn't drink our water or breathe our air cannot possibly represent us.

By presenting her opponent Joseph Crowley in a linguistically oppositional manner, the text communicates who Ocasio-Cortez is: someone who actually lives in NY-14.[2] After contending that under the incumbent's leadership New York changed to benefit developers and corporations at the detriment of the people (so, she is vying for a Congressional seat "to fight for a New York that working families can afford"), Ocasio-Cortez proclaims: "This race is about people versus money. We've got people, they've got money." With this dichotomy, Ocasio-Cortez accomplishes several things. First, she enacts the tactic of *distinction* – or "the identity relation of differentiation" (Bucholtz & Hall, 2005, p. 600) – with respect to Crowley: she highlights that her opponent accepts corporate campaign funds while she does not. Then, she creates an "us" versus "them" binary that situates her camp and campaign effort as grassroots and about the people, while Crowley's is based on monetary interests. Thus, she not only situates her opponent as a member of "the elite" (who have not met "the people's" demands) but she also reminds voters that in lieu of corporate money she has invested in a team of people who, like her, work hard to help her secure the nomination. The hard work motif is reinforced by the visuals of the campaign advertisement. As we listen to her narrating voice throughout the video, we see a day in the life of Ocasio-Cortez on her campaign trail that begins with getting ready in the morning before taking public transportation, engaging her future constituents, and speaking to an enthusiastic audience, and ends with a meal with her family. The quickly changing frames emphasize that a typical day for the candidate is teeming with physical movement and activity.

In summary, in the campaign advertisement, we see a candidate doing things that "regular" New Yorkers do: she travels by subway, changes from flats to heels on a subway platform, and sits among her family on a sofa to eat. As shown in the two images that constitute Figure 4.1, the candidate is often not pictured centrally and prominently in the frames of her campaign video. Instead, her image is offset. This portrayal is supportive of the broader identity work being accomplished in this video that involves adequating Ocasio-Cortez to NY-14, framing her as emblematic and representative of her community, and, therefore, building existential coherence through the strategy of a narrative of belonging (Duranti, 2006) founded on her (and also her family's) connection to the district and the manifold social categories that constitute her identity. This makes her final affirmation – "A New York for the many is possible. It's time for one of us" – and the final frame of the video, which shows the hashtag #OneOfUs alongside Ocasio-Cortez's campaign logo, ring true. The identity work performed in the video also involves the reconfiguration of aspects of her identity (e.g., non-white, non-wealthy, non-male) both as a political advantage through *illegitimation* processes and to suggest that, by pursuing her campaign,

The construction of Alexandria Ocasio-Cortez's political self

she has embarked on an onerous and intrepid endeavor, which serves to position the candidate within a larger (national and/or historical) storyline.

A tweeted narrative

This section turns to the narrative that Ocasio-Cortez told via the tweets she posted during her first Congressional campaign. Before exploring this narrative, an overview of these tweets is provided. Figure 4.2 displays the distribution of these tweets and conveys the frequency with which the candidate used the social media platform.

Across the full sample, excluding retweets, Ocasio-Cortez tweeted roughly seven times per day on average. However, Twitter was used differently in each phase of the campaign, with more frequent use before the primaries. Of the total tweets posted by during her first campaign, 3,334 tweets and an average of 8.1 tweets per day were posted during her primary campaign (from 17 May 2017 to 26 June 2018, before polls closed) and a total of 634 tweets and an average of only 5.0 tweets per day during the general election (from her primary win to 6 November 2018, before polls closed). This may be explained by the fact that, having secured the Democratic nomination after the primaries within a district that has elected a Democratic Representative since 1993, rigorous campaigning for the general election was not an exigency. The three peaks in usage, visible in Figure 4.2, all occur within the primary campaign: the

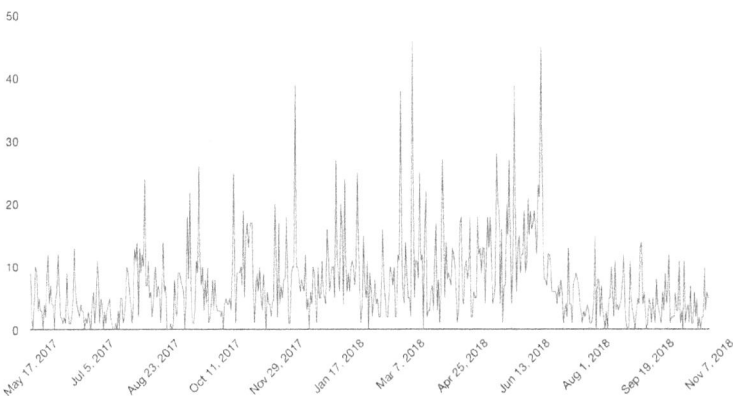

Figure 4.2 Frequency of @AOC tweets during the first Congressional campaign.

first, at the start of December 2017, coincided with a Twitter fundraiser; the second, in mid-March 2018, was followed a video featuring the candidate promoted by *Now This*, a popular progressive social media-focused news organization; and the third corresponds to Ocasio-Cortez's groundbreaking primary victory.

A community-based candidate from the Bronx

A closer look at the AOC first campaign corpus was provided via the identification of the most frequently used nouns using Sketch Engine, displayed in Table 4.1. What emerges from this analysis is a predictably high frequency of words related to the race, or "candidate," "campaign," "voter," and "election." The use of the terms "today," "time," "year," and "day" varied widely within the corpus. For instance, the temporal deictic "today" was used in Ocasio-Cortez's tweets not only to call attention to campaign events but it was also used to flag persisting human rights violations.

Unsurprisingly, this wordlist features many district-related terms, including "Bronx," "NYC," "NY," "Queens," and "NY-14." The less frequent occurrence of "NY" and "NYC" than the "Bronx" may be indicative of the desire to connect more directly with her constituents, and the more frequent occurrence of "Bronx" over "Queens" may reflect a yearning to highlight the candidate's borough of birth. The presence of these district-related terms, along with "people," "family," and "community," are suggestive of the candidate's attempt to position herself as a member of the community (among "the people") with deep roots in her district.

Table 4.1 Most frequent lemmas in the AOC first campaign corpus (nouns)

	Item	Freq		Item	Freq
1	People	359	11	Bronx	165
2	Time	248	12	Community	160
3	Candidate	244	13	NYC	155
4	Today	235	14	NY	151
5	Campaign	222	15	Day	146
6	Voter	185	16	Congress	144
7	Year	185	17	Election	142
8	Family	184	18	Queens	142
9	Ocasio2018	181	19	Woman	126
10	Money	168	20	NY-14	111

The construction of Alexandria Ocasio-Cortez's political self 47

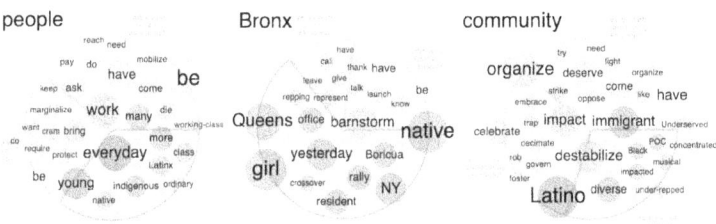

Figure 4.3 Word sketch visualization for "people," "Bronx," and "community."

To further explore this attempt, the word sketch function of Sketch Engine, which provides a visual summary of grammatical and collocational behavior of words (Kocincová et al., 2015), was applied to selected community-based terms including "people" (the most frequently used noun), "Bronx," and "community." The word sketch visualizations display selected relations by means of color clustering, as shown in Figure 4.3, with larger text sizes representing more frequent collocations.

These visuals are helpful because they make it possible for us to glean a lot of information quickly. First, with respect to Ocasio-Cortez's use of the word "people," as corroborated by the concordance tool, we see that it often co-occurs with "work," "everyday," and "young," suggesting that the people to whom Ocasio-Cortez is appealing are young, non-elite (or "everyday people"), workers, and/or part of the working class.

The term "Bronx," predictably, often co-occurs with Queens since parts of the two boroughs constitute the district. Less predictable are other frequently co-occurring words, or "native" and "girl." Of these, interestingly, the former is most often used with reference to others (such as Bronx-born City Council candidate Randy Abreu), while the latter is used by the candidate to define herself. Ocasio-Cortez's preference for the gendered noun in her self-portrayal is consistent with the frequent emergence of the noun "woman" in Ocasio-Cortez's campaign narrative on Twitter (as seen in Table 4.1) and can be viewed in the following tweets, in which the emphasis was added:

[…][3] This *Bronx girl* isn't pulling punches in Trump's America. I keep it 💯 in this convo too. […] 23 April 2018

[...] They've gone way too long to know how to handle a *Bronx girl* running for Congress 😉 24 May 2018

Here, the modifier "Bronx" is used to bring authenticity to facets of her character that the candidate aims to accentuate. In the first tweet excerpt, it is associated to not holding back ("not pulling punches") and being honest ("keep it 💯"), while in the second, to a bold and unpredictable outsider. By defining herself as a "Bronx girl," the candidate attempts to establish her credibility as a tough adversary that will not back down to the opposition, emblemized as "Trump's America."

Lastly, the collocates of "community" seen in the word sketch visualization narrate an association of the term primarily with "Latino" and "immigrant" populations, which also describe Ocasio-Cortez's heritage, who have been victimized by the "destabiliz[ing]" practices of the US Immigration and Customs Enforcement (ICE). The collocates also suggest the candidate's need and desire to "organize" and "impact" this "underserved" and "under-repped" community.

The use of territory-based referents, however, did more than just signal the candidate's membership in her community. As seen in the two tweets that follow, which cite the frequently used district-related terms "NYC," and "NY," her district was also occasioned with reference to its political shortfalls:

It's 2018. I am the ONLY female Congressional challenger in ALL of New York City. Only WOC ever to run in NY14. The NYC Dem culture is deeply broken. SO many insiders told me NOT to run. [...] 26 April 2018

[...] My niece walked into a Bronx bodega, stunned to see her *tía* on the wall [in a campaign poster]. NY-14 is a district that's 70% people of color. Due to NY laws that allow position inheritance, we've never had a non-White Congressmember. You can't be what you can't see. 18 April 2018

In these tweets, aspects of the identities that Ocasio-Cortez embodies (non-white, non-male, non-wealthy) are reconfigured as *illegitimated*, or "dismissed, censored, or simply ignored" (Bucholtz & Hall, 2005, p. 603), by the dominant structures of institutionalized power and ideology – "NYC Dem culture," "insiders," and "NY laws." The candidate suggests that the current system favors a type of person – white, male, and wealthy – that is not representative of the people of Queens and the Bronx. Thus, "the people," constituted by class-based, age, gender, racial, ethnic, and/or linguistic identities – as also suggested by the word sketch visualization for "people" in Figure 4.3 – is set against dominant structures and against "the elites" who uphold and perpetuate systems of under-representation, thereby damaging the diverse NY-14 community and threatening to stunt the (political) aspirations of young community members (i.e., "You can't be what you can't see").

Broadening the scope: Ocasio-Cortez's use of "our"

Pronoun use was also analyzed in the corpus of AOC first campaign tweets. As Chilton (2004) maintains, "in political discourse the first-person plural (we, us, our) can be used to induce interpreters to conceptualise group identity, coalitions, parties, and the like, either as insiders or as outsiders" (p. 56). Indeed, the possessive pronoun that most frequently occurs in the corpus is "our" (739 occurrences). To analyze the use of this pronoun, the concordance function of Sketch Engine was used to generate a random sample of 10 concordance lines in which "our" is the key word in context (KWIC), reproduced in chronological order in Table 4.2.

A close analysis of this output reveals that its meaning depends on the speaker and hearer's context-based "deictic positioning" (Chilton, 2004, p. 204; see also Filardo-Llamas & Boyd, 2018). Here, in addition to using "our" to index a team that is working on the campaign – an effort that certainly contributes to the motif of a grassroots and community-based movement that is constituted by large numbers of people who are advancing the candidate's campaign efforts – (concordance lines 1, 5, 7), the inclusive uses of the possessive pronoun index a progressively broadened audience within its referential scope, addressing the NY-14 community (2, 8), the constituents of the state of New York (3), and/or all Americans (4, 6, 9, 10).

Several linguistic strategies can be identified in these concordance results. The indexed community is made explicit through the use of location-specific words or phrases such as "Parkchester" (2), "Bronx" (8), and "in the United States of America" (10). Within the district-related examples, two often under-represented communities are referenced: in the first, on the occasion of the Muslim holiday Eid al-Adha, Ocasio-Cortez shows familiarity with the backgrounds of the communities within her district by citing "our Parkchester families" who celebrate the holiday (2), and in the

Table 4.2 Randomly generated sample of concordance results of "our" as KWIC

	Left	KWIC	Right	Date
1	Scouting locations for	our	June 24th Canvassing Kick-off!	6 June 2017
2	Eid Mubarak everyone! Love seeing	our	Parkchester families dressed to the nines today	1 September 2017
3	It is wrong to reward the IDC with co-leadership of the NY Senate and give GOP control of	our	budget when people voted for the opposite.	28 November 2017
4	Lead in our children's school water, lead on	our	walls. This is an urgent public health crisis. The money is there to fix it - as a nation we've spent constantly on tax cuts for the rich and fighter jets (but not veteran care).	16 December 2017
5	If you're not local, phonebank via [url] (that's	our	campaign dialer) or give at [url].	17 January 2018
6	As Americans,	our	destinies are tied much closer than we think. Vulture capital funds are perfecting their predatory behaviors in #PuertoRico	27 January 2018
7	Thank you [@username]!	Our	team worked really hard to define our mission. Folks can learn more at [url]	30 May 2018
8	Had a blast at Bronx Pride with	our	LGBT+ family today!	18 June 2018
9	The fact that my platform is called "radical" is more a reflection of	our	current political moment & how far we've strayed from our bold, visionary past.	4 July 2018
10	This administration stands against	our	most basic values of freedom, justice, and self-expression in the United States.	21 October 2018

second, following her participation in the Bronx Pride Festival, the candidate explicitly references "our LGBT+ family" (8). The use of the lemma "family" in these two cases has differing functions, but both emphasize belonging: in the first, it refers to literal nuclear families, and the use of "our" underscores their belonging to the NY-14 community, while the use of "family" in the latter case emphasizes the sense of belonging already occasioned by the use of "our." In the two cases, "our" expresses the candidate's closeness to these groups.

In addition to these very specific references, Ocasio-Cortez's tweets also present a more global appeal to the American people. In concordance line 6, the destinies to which Ocasio-Cortez refers are those of Americans living in the continental United States *and* in Puerto Rico. Thus, by beginning her tweet with "as Americans," she underscores that Puerto Ricans are as American as inhabitants of the continental United States, which is a factual yet politically charged statement. In examples 9 and 10, the "current political moment," "bold, visionary past," and "most basic values of freedom, justice, and self-expression" are shared with all of the American people. It is noteworthy that these two tweets were both posted subsequent to her primary win, so by using this more ambiguous referent Ocasio-Cortez is inhabiting a less local, more national political persona, more consonant with her role as a US Representative.

Ocasio-Cortez's emoji use

Another feature of Ocasio-Cortez's tweets is the use of symbols and emoji, for which frequencies are displayed in Table 4.3. Ocasio-Cortez used the purple heart emoji more frequently than any other lemma listed in Table 4.2. Only the dollar sign ($) and the percentage sign (%) were used more frequently, in absolute terms, in the 1,022,146-token Reference corpus of Representatives' tweets (which was over 8 times larger than Ocasio-Cortez's campaign corpus). These two signs can serve as evidence of the strategy through which politicians draw on figures and statistics to legitimize their claims (Reyes, 2011). Furthermore, in general, these digital pictographs serve as a way to circumvent Twitter's character limit, as many emoji stand in for words or phrases, or have deictic functions, such as the downward arrow emoji – the second most frequent emoji in the AOC first campaign corpus – often used to function like a deictic verb, pointing to text or images that follows. However, they hold multitudinous other functions as well.

Table 4.3 Most frequently used symbols and emoji

	Symbol	Name	Freq		Symbol	Name	Freq
1	💜	Purple heart	368	11		Sparkles	32
2	⬇	Downward arrow	218	12	☎	Telephone	31
3	$	Dollar sign	140	13		Face with tears of joy	30
4	%	Percentage sign	128	14		Woman gesturing no	29
5	💪	Flexed biceps	122	15		Clapping hands	29
6	💰	Money bag	71	16		Flag of the United States	26
7	😉	Winking face	67	17		Hugging face	24
8	✅	Check mark button	56	18		Police car light	19
9		Flag of Puerto Rico	51	19	🔥	Fire	19
10		Ballot box	45	20		Raised fist	19

Ocasio-Cortez adopted purple as the color of her campaign, so the purple heart serves as an emblem copiously inserted within her campaign tweets to reinforce her campaign message and, essentially, her brand. Oftentimes, it followed expressions of gratitude in replies to constituents. In roughly one-third of its instances, the purple heart occurred immediately before or after the flexed biceps emoji,[4] as in the following examples that illustrate excerpts of tweets:

Juntos sí podemos 💜💪 24 October 2017

Thanks again for your support 💜💪 09 November 2017

Grassroots energy comes from that. Real recognize real. 💪💜 13 November 2017

The message that is dispensed in these tweets conveys strength in numbers and connects support for the campaign with strength (*Juntos sí podemos* "together yes we can," "support," and "grassroots energy"). This notion was taken up in the candidate's campaign advertisement in which her Congressional race is equated to a courageous feat.

The construction of Alexandria Ocasio-Cortez's political self 53

Importantly, like the fourteenth, fifteenth, and twentieth most frequently used emoji, the flexed biceps emoji used by Ocasio-Cortez is modified by skin tone, and the race-neutral yellow emoji depicting the same action accounts for less than 10% of occurrences. In their study of user interpretations of skin-tone modifiers, Sweeney and Whaley (2019) found that these modifiers made "race an explicit variable and part of communication" (n.p.). The use of skin-tone modified emoji heightens visibility of and serves to direct attention to identity features that users want to accentuate. In this light, it can be argued these emoji used by Ocasio-Cortez function as salient markers and reminders of her belonging to the Latinx community.

Another frequently used skin-tone modified emoji was the clapping hands emoji. The following examples show that the candidate uses this emoji not only to applaud commendable actions but also for emphasis after each word:

> […] This is what intersectionality looks like: @CaribEquality's LGBTQ+ 🌈 Celebration in Queens hosted presentations on *both* immigration status AND being out & Muslim. Incredible, incredible work! 👏💜 25 February 2018

> Last year @repjoecrowley, the Queens Dems chairman, worked to bump EVERY 👏WOMAN 👏OFF 👏THE BALLOT 👏 in City Council race 21, so his protégé could cakewalk into the seat. The lack of women in NYC government isn't an accident. It's by design. 08 May 2018

> Don't 👏 trust 👏 Corporate 👏 Democrats 👏 in 2018 👏 They rake in TONS of big pharma 💰 while co-signing every Bernie bill in existence, until they get a majority back. […] 16 May 2018

In the first tweet, Ocasio-Cortez inserts the clapping hands emoji as a positive evaluation that reinforces the preceding text "Incredible, incredible work!" and is followed by her symbol, the purple heart emoji, which here serves as further endorsement of the Caribbean Equality Project's events. The second and third tweets instead use the clapping hands emoji as a beat gesture, with a set of consecutive words each followed by the emoji. This beat-related use of the emoji, which has off-line African American origins (Gawne & McCulloch, 2019), serves to emphasize the message – further accentuated with all caps in the second tweet – that Crowley, who is mentioned by name and by his title, acted deliberately to keep women out of elected office and that "Corporate Democrats" are deceitful and corrupt. Interestingly, instead of using a single skin-tone, the third tweet adds employs emoji of different skin tones, indicative of the attempt to be inclusive and representative. The sixth most frequently used emoji was the money bag. In Ocasio-Cortez's campaign tweets, this symbol substituted for the word "money" in instances in which she wished to stress the money that her opponent and other politicians accepted:

> That is why I will not take special interest 💰. Compromising my responsibilities to protecting our families and future isn't worth it. 31 May 2017
>
> I was stopped and recognized TWICE this morning [...] It usually costs campaigns tons of 💰 to get that kind of name ID. We're doing it by knocking on 1000s of doors, often and early. 21 February 2018
>
> My opponent has already spent $3 million dollars, and raised more 💰 from GOP lobbyists this week. [...] 22 June 2018

In the first tweet, the candidate delegitimizes special interest funding, to which attention is directed with the use of the emoji, on the grounds that it undermines the well-being of "our families" and their future. In the second tweet, the emoji is again used to emphasize money, but this time, it is set against the physical effort that Ocasio-Cortez and her team are doing to gain recognition. Evoking producerism and the Protestant ethic, the hard work that has been dedicated to the campaign underpins her (potential for) success, rather than "big money." The third tweet, which chastises Crowley, uses the emoji to stand in for money collected from lobbyists loyal to the GOP, across the political aisle. The money bag emoji, therefore, refers to corrupting money from special interest groups and lobbyists that is used to cast a negative light on her immoral opponents and to position herself as ethical and hardworking.

It is also noteworthy that the flag of Puerto Rico is present in the AOC first campaign corpus roughly twice as often as the flag of the US emoji. In four instances, the two flag emoji appeared in the same tweet. Ocasio-Cortez's sparse usage of the US flag emoji is remarkable when considering that the national flag emerged as the third most used emoji in the tweets of members of the House of Representatives of the 115th and 116th US Congress, analyzed in Kariryaa et al. (2020). In the study, however, the researchers did find that parties and politicians on the right used the national flag emoji more frequently than those on the left, which might in part explain Ocasio-Cortez's nonfrequent usage of the US flag (Kariryaa et al., 2020).

Why, instead, did Ocasio-Cortez include the flag of Puerto Rico emoji so frequently in her tweets? An analysis of the tweets in which the flag of Puerto Rico appears reveals that the emoji was usually used at the end of tweets that referred to the unincorporated US territory or immediately following reference to its name or its inhabitants, as seen in the following examples:

> I don't want your prayers, @JoeCrowleyNY. I want you to undo the horrendous PROMESA Act that sold our families to the highest bidder 🇵🇷 21 September 2017
>
> 700,000 New Yorkers of Puerto Rican descent, many in #thebronx. Congress, pass #PuertoRicoRelief now. We did it for Harvey, do it for PR. 🇵🇷 26 September 2017
>
> I cannot tell you how intensely frustrating it is as a member of the #Boricua 🇵🇷 diaspora, my family on the island breathing air full of fungal spores because no one is fixing rotting homes […] 08 June 2018
>
> Can't help but reflect this Election Day: as my family in Puerto Rico watches me run for Congress, they still don't have the right to vote in federal elections - despite being subject to federal lawmakers. 🇵🇷🌺 […] 06 November 2018

In all but one of these four tweets, Ocasio-Cortez explicitly occasions her Puerto Rican heritage ("our families," "as a member of the #Boricua 🇵🇷 diaspora" and "my family on the island," and "my family in Puerto Rico"). These tweets underscore how current US Representatives have failed Puerto Rico, in terms of backing and implementing unfair financial policies (PROMESA), reluctance to provide humanitarian aid in the aftermath of Hurricane Maria – the Hurricane that had a deadly impact when it struck Puerto Rico and neighboring islands in 2017, and upholding the lack of voting representation in the US Federal government. Seen in this light, the emoji that recurs in these tweets serves to draw attention to the fact that the candidate has cited Puerto Rico, and to reinforce both her familial connection to the island and her commitment to implementing policies that favor and defend its people.

In short, Ocasio-Cortez displays an artful use of emoji that index and occasion different aspects of her identity, campaign, and platform, and display how these three aspects are interconnected. Although skillful use of these non-textual features is useful to adhere to Twitter's character limit, there is evidence that the Representative uses these resources not just as substitutions for words but to draw attention to specific connotations (like corrupt money accepted by immoral politicians) or features (like inclusive skin-tone modified emoji). Recurrent emoji use further serves as a method to create coherence in her tweeted narrative: the purple heart symbolizes her campaign, the skin-tone modified emoji index her identity as a person of color, the Puerto Rican flag both places emphasis on her heritage and on her willingness to fight for Puerto Rico.

Comparative keyword analysis: Ocasio-Cortez and other representatives

Although reference has already been made to some differences in how Ocasio-Cortez communicated on Twitter compared to other politicians, comparative keyword analysis was performed to explore this aspect further, more systematically. This analysis was conducted using Sketch Engine to generate the list of keywords, contained in Table 4.4. The top 30 keywords are arranged by their *keyness*, which is a construct that relates to how unusual the frequency of a given term is within a corpus (Gabrielatos, 2018).

Predictably, the top results of this analysis include terms specifically related to Ocasio-Cortez's campaign (e.g., Ocasio2018; Ocasio-Cortez), and her district (e.g., NY-14, Queens, Bronx, BX,

Table 4.4 Results of the comparative keyword analysis

	Item	Freq	Keyness		Item	Freq	Keyness
1	Ocasio2018	188	1545.300	16	Hermana	12	99.570
2	NY-14	119	978.510	17	BNC	12	99.570
3	Crowley	57	469.220	18	PR	59	98.840
4	Queens	142	394.850	19	JD	20	83.550
5	Bronx	165	344.690	20	Bilingual	10	83.140
6	BX	36	296.720	21	Corona	10	83.140
7	Ocasio-Cortez	25	206.360	22	Luxury	28	78.130
8	IDC	24	198.140	23	Tuition-free	22	61.460
9	Yep	20	165.290	24	Hop	29	60.790
10	Rikers	17	140.640	25	Yup	12	50.330
11	BOE	14	116.000	26	Ambitious	12	50.330
12	Dialer	13	107.790	27	Bodega	11	46.180
13	Developer	25	104.310	28	Electorate	11	46.180
14	PROMESA	12	99.570	29	EST	16	44.79
15	Pollsite	12	99.570	30	María	10	42.03

Corona). Other keywords are specialized, policy-related terms, including "IDC" (Independent Democratic Conference), "BOE" (Board of Elections), and "PROMESA" (Puerto Rico Oversight, Management, and Economic Stability Act). Given that this corpus is being compared to that of other lawmakers, the emergence of these terms is less suggestive of a high degree of specialization of her Twitter discourse and more indicative of Ocasio-Cortez's aim to advance her people-centered and left-wing populist-leaning platform (in which, for instance, she advocates for "tuition-free" higher education and affordable housing against "luxury" "developer[s]") and to fight for Puerto Rico – or "PR" – also signaled by her mention of Hurricane "María." Undoubtedly, the use of these specialized terms serves the purpose of legitimating her discourse, and of positioning herself as an adept politician. Two additional acronyms, or "BNC" (Brand New Congress, an American political action committee) and "JD" (Justice Democrats), act as political identity markers and situate Ocasio-Cortez as a Democratic Socialist, outside of the realm of establishment politicians.

Terms signaling her political identity co-occur with others that mark her socioeconomic and ethnic identity. Notable, in fact, are the presence on this list of "bodega" and "María." Bodega is the name assigned to corner stores in New York City and, although many other ethnic groups have opened bodegas, they remain closely associated with Puerto Ricans (Lo Wang, 2017). Thus, citing this business is a way for Ocasio-Cortez to connect to her district and its Puerto Rican community. "María" does not only index a connection to Puerto Rico in the sense suggested earlier, but it could be argued that the use of the acute accent in the name signals it as non-English or it is, at least, Hispanicized, seeing as the Hurricane name was written without the accent by government agencies.[5] This orthography – along with, of course, "hermana" and "bilingual" – acts as visual identity markers that position Ocasio-Cortez as a member of the Latinx and Puerto Rican communities.

Another category of words that transpires in this comparative keyword analysis is single affirmative words, or "yep" and "yup." These words, which fit within the domain of informal, online talk, are used in reply to other tweets instead of the standard equivalent "yes." Ocasio-Cortez's higher usage of these terms in comparison with other Representatives along with her use of emoji discussed earlier is suggestive of Ocasio-Cortez's willingness to engage in informal online talk, which fashions a style that characterizes her written communications during her campaign (and even after her election, as will be discussed in Chapter 6).

In summary, the analysis of tweets suggests that, during her first political campaign, Ocasio-Cortez presented an image of herself via her tweets that emphasized facets of her identity that situated the candidate as a member of the community: she is a "Bronx girl," a Puerto Rican, and ultimately a candidate who is in-touch with the needs of the community. Her communicative style – characterized by frequent and artful use of emoji – frames her as different from traditional, establishment politicians whose discourse is formal and less accessible, and positions her as antiestablishment. Notwithstanding the projection of an "of the people" and "for the people" political persona, the analysis of pronouns suggests a desire to reach a progressively broadened audience that includes all of the American people, thereby channeling a political identity that extends beyond the bounds of NY-14.

Narrating Alexandria Ocasio-Cortez: novelty and populism in her campaign ad and tweets

With reference to presidential candidate John McCain, Parry-Giles and Steudeman (2017) argue that, to voters, McCain's platform and policy prescriptions "only mattered insofar as they emanated from that candidate's political identity, the composite image the candidate so delicately crafted amid the constant churn of the political campaign" (p. 82). Even though much has been written about Trump's character-centric rhetoric, through which he achieved "authenticity" and exploited both social media and the 24-hour news cycle (e.g., Enli, 2017), Parry-Giles and Steudeman (2017) maintain that McCain preceded Trump in the understanding that political identity construction was a worthy endeavor. I argue that Alexandria Ocasio-Cortez followed in these footsteps, but she did so by using the set of tools at her disposal differently and skillfully.

This chapter, in fact, did not examine the policies and campaign promises advanced by Ocasio-Cortez in her effort to convince voters to elect her as US Representative. It instead focused on the story of Ocasio-Cortez the candidate, as a character whose plot was constituted by selected life events and whose setting was her district. Rather than a complex assemblage of past situations and events, Ocasio-Cortez stitched together a simple, coherent narrative that crafted her political identity and made a case for her candidacy.

Recounting her identity in this way made her campaign *about* her identity. Both the campaign video and her tweets strove to position the candidate as a member of her community and to illustrate a profound connection to her district that was not only physical, emotional, and moral but also bound to her personal and family history. Emblematized by her campaign hashtag #OneOfUs, Ocasio-Cortez's Twitter feed and campaign ad developed a campaign narrative of a nonestablishment candidate who "actually" lived in her district, took public transportation, refused corporate donations, and foregrounded the needs of her community. This narrative served to frame her opponent Joseph Crowley as an integral member of the out-of-touch, profiteering Washington establishment.

Ocasio-Cortez's personal narrative as a working-class Bronxite with deep ties to her community situated her as one of "us" ("the people") fighting for the working class against an incumbent slated to become the next Speaker of the House. In her campaign ad, she states: "we've got people, they've got money." In this light, her campaign could be viewed as constructing an opposition based primarily on class, in line with her social-democratic views (Georgiou, 2020), and as striving for a victory of "the people" (the diverse working-class community of her district) against a member of "the elite" (a finance-driven insider) who was unwilling and/or unable to fulfill "the people's" demands. The class-based populist overtones are further symbolized by the money bag emoji used to stand in for the corrupt money that other compromised politicians willfully accepted.

Although the class-based division is the most evident us-versus-them binary enacted by Ocasio-Cortez's narrative, also bolstered by her Democratic Socialist platform, there are additional identity facets that the candidate occasions in the search for adequation with her constituents and difference from her opponents. Her intersectional identity was placed at the forefront in her groundbreaking campaign ad most palpably with its initial utterance "Women like me aren't supposed to run for office," and the message that she is one of the diverse (in terms of class, age, gender, racial, ethnic, and/or linguistic identities) and underrepresented "people" reverberates throughout her tweeted narrative as well. This is not only conveyed in the content of her tweets but also in the discursive devices she adopts.

Kazin (2017) holds that "the most basic and telling definition of populism" is "a language whose speakers conceive of ordinary people as a noble assemblage not bounded narrowly by class, view their elite opponents as self-serving and undemocratic, and seek to mobilize the former against the latter" (p. 1). Ocasio-Cortez uses this language to present herself as an aspiring leader who is at once of the people and for the people. The widespread use of less formal, popular channels such as Twitter itself allowed Ocasio-Cortez to cast herself not only as a representative of but also as the voice of the people. Crucially, the narrative work that accomplished this framing and advanced a left-wing populist discourse was enacted not only in the story that Ocasio-Cortez told but also in *how* she told it. Her campaign video helps her move stealthily between presenting herself as ordinary and extraordinary: it depicts her doing what ordinary New Yorkers do but, as encapsulated by the title of the video, she has the political courage it takes to change the system.

Another related critical thread in the candidate's narrative was the effort she made to authenticate her identity and situate her campaign as founded on hard work and social justice, in congruence with historical or archetypal figures, enacted by frequent references to her intersectional identity, to the diversity of her district, to the needs of communities within her district, and to the hard work – versus corrupt money – that propelled her campaign. This narrative was crafted discursively and multimodally, with careful details that embellished and reinforced its coherence, such as by using skin-tone modified emoji and non-English orthography such as the acute accent. Her crafted persona – as the embodiment of social reform and representation within her district against a profiteering member of the "elite" – dwarfed her policies. Her pronoun use suggests that Ocasio-Cortez aimed to inhabit a less local, more national political persona particularly after her primary win, in accordance with her forthcoming role as a member of the US House of Representatives. Together, the features present in her campaign ad and tweets that showed both evidence of traditional political discourse and great innovation naturalized the link among her decision to run, her past experiences, and her desire to defeat a self-serving opponent for the well-being of her community. They also fashioned a style that positioned her as young and approachable, and reinforced her campaign brand.

In the next chapter, we home in on the opposition attacks levied against Representative Ocasio-Cortez both in mainstream media content and user-generated content that threatened the coherence of the personal narrative and political self that she so carefully crafted during her first campaign.

Notes

1 Blommaert (2019) suggests that Ocasio-Cortez echoes Trump's 'Drain the Swamp' campaign message: like Trump, she can capitalize from outsider status because outsiders have the transformative potential to change the system. Importantly, however, Ocasio-Cortez is dissimilar to Trump because she can more credibly position herself as an insider in her community.
2 When, on 2 May 2018, a civil rights lawyer asked candidates on Twitter to explain why they were qualified for their position in three words or less, Ocasio-Cortez replied: "I (actually) live here", stressing that her opponent did not.
3 In the interest of conciseness, in this chapter tweets are sometimes shortened, and omitted text is represented by […].
4 In all but 12 instances, the flexed biceps emoji was included in tweets before or after the purple heart emoji.
5 For instance, a September 2017 National Oceanic and Atmospheric Administration and National Weather Service report (https://www.nhc.noaa.gov/data/tcr/AL152017_Maria.pdf, updated in 2019) was titled "Hurricane Maria."

References

Blommaert, J. (2019). Alexandria Ocasio-Cortez: The next level of political digital culture, *Diggit Magazine*, https://medium.com/@diggitmagazine/alexandria-ocasio-cortez-the-next-level-of-political-digital-culture-e43b45518e86
Bucholtz, M. & Hall, K. (2005). Identity and interaction: A socio-cultural linguistic approach. *Discourse Studies*, 7(4–5), 585–614.
Chilton, P.A. (2004). *Analysing Political Discourse: Theory and Practice*. London-New York: Routledge.
Duranti, A. (2006). Narrating the political self in a campaign for U.S. Congress. *Language in Society*, 35(4), 467–497.
Enli, G. (2017). Twitter as arena for the authentic outsider: Exploring the social media campaigns of Trump and Clinton in the 2016 US presidential election. *European Journal of Communication*, 32(1), 50–61.
Filardo-Llamas, L. & Boyd, M.S. (2018). Critical discourse analysis and politics. In J. Flowerdew & J. E. Richardson (Eds.), *The Routledge Handbook of Critical Discourse Studies* (pp. 312–327). London-New York: Routledge.
Gabrielatos, C. (2018). Keyness analysis: Nature, metrics and techniques. In C. Taylor & A. Marchi (Eds.), *Corpus Approaches to Discourse* (pp. 225–258). London-New York: Routledge.
Gawne, L. & McCulloch, G. (2019). Emoji as digital gestures. *Language@Internet*, 17(2) https://www.languageatinternet.org/articles/2019/gawne
Georgiou, N. (2020). Alexandria Ocasio-Cortez's Populism and Relatability. *Diggit Magazine*, Retrieved from: https://www.diggitmagazine.com/articles/alexandria-ocasio-cortezs-populism-and-relatability

Kariryaa, A., et al. (2020). The role of flag emoji in online political communication. *Social Science Computer Review*, 40(2), 367–387.

Kazin, M. (2017). *The Populist Persuasion: An American History*. Ithaca-London: Cornell University Press.

Kilgarriff, A. (2009). Simple maths for keywords. In M. Mahlberg, V. González-Díaz and C. Smith (Eds.), *Proceedings of Corpus Linguistics Conference CL2009*, University of Liverpool, UK.

Kilgarriff, A. et al. (2014). The sketch engine: Ten years on. *Lexicography ASIALEX*, 1, 7–36.

Kocincová, L. et al. (2015). Interactive Visualizations of Corpus Data in Sketch Engine. *NEALT Proceedings Series*, 25(3), 17–22.

Lo Wang, H. (2017). New York City Bodegas and the generations who love them, *NPR*, Retrieved from: https://www.npr.org/sections/codeswitch/2017/03/10/518376170/new-york-city-bodegas-and-the-generations-who-love-them

Mackay, R.R. (2013). Multimodal legitimation: Looking at and listening to Obama's ads. In P. Cap & U. Okulska (Eds.), *Analyzing Genres in Political Communication: Theory and Practice* (pp. 345–377). Amsterdam-Philadelphia: John Benjamins.

Meade, M. & Robles, J. (2017). Historical and existential coherence in political commercials. *Discourse & Communication*, 11(4), 404–432.

Parry-Giles, T. & Steudeman, M.J. (2017). Crafting character, moving history: John McCain's political identity in the 2008 presidential campaign. *Quarterly Journal of Speech*, 103(1–2), 66–89.

Reyes, A. (2011). Strategies of legitimization in political discourse: From words to actions. *Discourse & Society*, 22(6), 781–807.

Sclafani, J. (2018). Performing politics. In R. Wodak & B. Forchtner (Eds.), *The Routledge Handbook of Language and Politics* (pp. 398–411). Oxon-New York: Routledge.

Schubert, C. (2021). Multimodal cohesion in persuasive discourse: A case study of televised campaign advertisements in the 2020 US presidential election. *Discourse, Context & Media*, 43, 1–10.

Scott, M. (1997). PC analysis of key words—And key key words. *System*, 25, 233–245.

Sweeney, M.E. & Whaley, K. (2019). Technically white: Emoji skin-tone modifiers as American technoculture. *First Monday*, 24(7), np.

Watkins, S.C. (2019). *Don't Knock the Hustle*. Boston: Beacon Press.

Wrubel, L. & Kerchner, D. (2020). 116th U.S. Congress Tweet Ids. *Harvard Dataverse*, V1.

5 Attacks on a progressive newcomer
Fox News coverage and its uptake online

The anti-AOC offensive

Since taking office, Representative Ocasio-Cortez has borne the brunt of intense criticism from across the political aisle. In July 2019, former US President Donald Trump (in)famously suggested in a series of tweets that the Representative and her freshmen Progressive colleagues – namely, Representatives Ilhan Omar of Minnesota, Rashida Tlaib of Michigan, and Ayanna Pressley of Massachusetts – "go back" and try to fix the "totally broken crime infested places" they "originally came from" before telling "the people of the United States, the greatest and most powerful Nation on earth" how to run the US government. These tweets were widely condemned for their racist overtones toward these Progressive Representatives who are all women of color, all but one born in the United States, and all American citizens. Yet, albeit grounded in fallacious premises, this public condemnation by the leader of the United States toward US Representatives was of great impact. It positioned these lawmakers as "the other" and illegitimated their identity as elected government officials based chiefly on their non-white status.

A year later, political website *The Hill* ran a story about Representative Ocasio-Cortez that garnered significant attention. It claimed that Ted Yoho, a Republican US Representative from Florida, called Ocasio-Cortez a sexist slur outside the Capitol building. In the article, Ocasio-Cortez declared that she "never had" this "kind of disrespect levied at" her (Lillis, 2020). The next day, Yoho took to the House floor to deliver a response. In his speech, he referenced his wife and daughters as evidence that he did not use the alleged offensive language. Yoho neither apologized nor called Ocasio-Cortez by name. The incident and its aftermath were covered internationally and treated as emblematic of the discrimination and misogyny experienced by women in power.

DOI: 10.4324/9781003273103-5

Representative Ocasio-Cortez had already claimed the spotlight with her bootstrapping ascent, her upset win, and her social media presence, but the opposition attacks that she endured served as springboards that catapulted Ocasio-Cortez to fame and widespread notoriety. Before analyzing how the Representative responded to them (an aim of Chapter 6), this chapter examines the nature of these attacks with a focus on one of Ocasio-Cortez's earliest and most vociferous critics: the Fox News network, the mainstream media bastion of American conservativism, and right-wing populism (see Chapter 2).

One of the main concerns of this chapter is the context of discourse, where context is understood as "the totality of conditions under which discourse is being produced, circulated and interpreted" (Blommaert, 2005, p. 251). Thus, Fox News coverage of Ocasio-Cortez is examined from different perspectives. First, widely viewed excerpts of Fox News shows dedicated to Ocasio-Cortez and posted on YouTube are analyzed both in terms of the discursive strategies that were used in the delegitimization and other-presentation of the Representative and how they are reflective of greater (e.g., right-wing populist) discourses. Next, the transformation of excerpts of Ocasio-Cortez's political discourse as they were extracted from their original context and inserted into the new context of Fox News segments is examined along with the effects of this recontextualization. Finally, a corpus of online user comments is analyzed to see how the messages dispensed in Fox News coverage of the Representative are taken up and elaborated by users.

Methods

Selected news segments

To study Fox News attacks on Representative Ocasio-Cortez, the ten most viewed Fox News YouTube videos centered on the lawmaker were selected. This approach was chosen for several reasons. First, the video sharing service affords the opportunity to have more targeted information from viewers. YouTube provides not only view counts essential for the identification of the most viewed videos about a given topic (e.g., Ocasio-Cortez) but also additional metadata including the like/dislike count and user comments. Moreover, the Fox News videos uploaded to YouTube usually consist of only a focused excerpt of the full programs of which the topic is generally noted in the title. This increases the likelihood that the selected videos attracted viewers because of the subject at hand.

YouTube was searched at the start of 2022 to identify the top stories posted by the official Fox News channel (https://www.youtube.com/c/FoxNews) that covered and/or discussed Ocasio-Cortez. To retrieve these videos, a search on the official channel for the Representative's name ("AOC" or "Ocasio-Cortez") was performed and the ten videos with the most views were identified. One video segment in which Ocasio-Cortez was not the primary focus was excluded from the analysis. Once the videos were selected, they were carefully transcribed.

The titles assigned to the segments, the date in which the video was posted, and the view, like (to the nearest 1,000), and comment counts as of 15 March 2022 of the top ten videos are included in Table 5.1. The numeration (1–10) is used to reference each segment throughout the chapter.

The analysis of the transcripts was driven by CDA in its attempt to analyze how delegitimization and other-presentation are constructed in discourse. A first round of analysis revolved around the four categories for the critical analysis of the construction of (de)legitimization in discourse delineated in van Leeuwen (2008, pp. 105–106), or mythopoesis, authorization, rationalization, and moral evaluation (see Chapter 3). A second round centered on the five discourse-historical discursive macro-strategies, or nomination, predication, argumentation, perspectivization, and mitigation and intensification (Reisigl & Wodak, 2009).

A subsequent analytical step homed in on the "Tucker Carlson Tonight" segment entitled "Ocasio-Cortez lashes out at unflattering likability poll." This segment was selected for further analysis because, as indicated in Table 5.1, it accrued significantly more views than other videos and, therefore, posed an interesting subject of investigation. The purpose of this analysis was to examine the processes that determined the recontextualization of Ocasio-Cortez's speech, something that recurred throughout this excerpt. To provide additional insights, this segment included additional transcription conventions: (.) indicates pauses, underlined text designates stressed words, and brackets denote embodied practices and video conventions. The analysis of this video focused on the transformation of four excerpts of Ocasio-Cortez's political discourse as they were extracted from their original context and inserted into the segment, and the effects of this recontextualization. To this end, it drew on Fairclough's (2003) "recontextualizing principles" – presence,

Table 5.1 Most viewed videos about Representative Ocasio-Cortez from the official Fox News YouTube channel

	Title	Posted on	View count	Like count	Comments
1	Ocasio-Cortez lashes out at unflattering likability poll	20 March 2019	5,315,898	103K	20,467
2	Watters: This was Ocasio-Cortez's downfall	1 February 2022	3,064,896	82K	15,185
3	Shapiro on Ocasio-Cortez claiming to have Jewish heritage	12 December 2018	3,055,420	43K	7,522
4	Shapiro sounds off on Ocasio-Cortez Twitter exchange	10 August 2018	2,862,693	50K	9,236
5	DeSantis hits Ocasio-Cortez: I don't care if she's an Eskimo	25 July 2018	2,719,322	46K	10,137
6	Hannity: Ocasio-Cortez bashes capitalism	12 March 2019	2,713,785	28K	11,352
7	Barstool Sports founder reacts to AOC calling him out	15 August 2019	2,600,676	31K	3,711
8	Tomi Lahren: I love seeing Ocasio-Cortez on TV	23 July 2018	2,399,812	28K	13,602
9	Tucker: It's hard to believe this is happening in America	10 April 2021	2,342,399	78K	15,088
10	Tucker shreds AOC for demanding relief money go to illegal immigrants	28 March 2020	2,234,093	44K	Turned off

abstraction, arrangement, and additions – as an interpretative key to analyze how elements of her discourse were selectively "filtered" in representations across contexts (see Chapter 3).

The YouTube comments posted in response to this video were also analyzed. 20,467 comments written in the three-year time frame between 20 March 2019 and 20 March 2022[1] were extracted from YouTube. The comments constituted a 401,957-word (467,543-token[2]) corpus that was analyzed using Sketch Engine (www.sketchengine.eu). Lexical analysis was done by means of keyness analysis, a lexical extraction technique performed to identify the most relevant words in the comment corpus. This method involves comparing the frequency lists of two corpora – a larger and more general reference corpus, and a smaller and more specialized target corpus – to develop a list of keywords. For this study, the reference corpus, readily available in Sketch Engine, was English Web 2020 (enTenTen20; Jakubíček et al., 2013), constituted by texts collected from the Internet between 2019 and 2021. This corpus contains sub-corpora based on language varieties and – considering the topic of the YouTube video and the likely linguacultural background of commenting users – the sub-corpora "US domain.us," with roughly 353 million words, was used as a reference corpus for the keyness analysis. The list of keywords generated, reproduced in Table 5.2, excludes the names Alexandria Ocasio-Cortez and Tucker Carlson.

Next, the concordance lines with "she is a," or the most frequent 3–4-gram or sequence of 3–4 items in the corpus, which occurred 478 times, were analyzed. To look more closely at this formulation, given the significant number of occurrences and in light of space constraints, Sketch Engine was used to generate a random sample of five concordance lines. This approach was taken to reduce the number of concordance lines to a manageable number while preserving the representativeness of the sample. The analysis of these five concordance lines concerned the ways in which commenters appropriated, co-constructed, and rescaled the content of the Fox News video to which they were commenting.

Dismantling legitimacy on Fox News

The top ten most viewed Fox News excerpts on YouTube that focused on Representative Ocasio-Cortez are presented and analyzed in the following sections. They detail the mechanisms used across all ten of the excerpts to enact negative other-presentation and, more prominently, the delegitimization of the antagonist. The next sections each foreground a delegitimization category – or mythopoesis and authorization, respectively – though reference to all four categories are included in each section since, as van Leeuwen (2007) indicates, these forms of (de)legitimization often occur in combination.

Ocasio-Cortez as un- and anti-American

One of the strategies employed by Fox News hosts in their effort to delegitimize Ocasio-Cortez is mythopoesis through the use of cautionary tales. In these tales, as seen in the four excerpts from "Your World" (a), "Hannity" (b), and "Tucker Carlson Tonight" (c and d), Ocasio-Cortez is depicted as un-American, a common propagandist device used in the United States (Skidmore, 2015), and, more poignantly, as anti-American, deliberately working against the best interests of the American people. If her actions are allowed and/or policies are enacted, the imagined future is at best undesirable and at worst a "nightmare scenario" (Ross & Rivers, 2017):

a   One of the things that has always made us great is an appreciation for some kind of intellectual diversity, right? Being able to have civil debates, being able to share ideas. I mean, that's how we evolve, that's how we get better. But when one side isn't even willing to have the conversation, where does that leave us as a country? (segment 4)
b   Ocasio-Cortez the new radical extreme Socialist Democrat enlightening the crowd at the South by Southwest festival by calling Reagan a racist, FDR a racist, suggesting the United States is based on a garbage system. And she wants you, the American people, to hand over the keys to your private businesses, your private property. [...] According to her, her government knows best. Not you, not we, not the American people. Not the people who risk, reward, incentive, and create goods and services that make our lives easier and better, that people want, need, and desire. She and her colleagues know better. (6)
c   Ocasio-Cortez is one of the largest political megaphones on earth. But she wants more than that. She now insists that not only should she be able to speak totally unfiltered to millions of people at once but that nobody should be allowed to disagree with what she says. [...] Here you have one of the most powerful politicians in America using the most powerful companies in the world to censor her political opponents. That sounds like authoritarianism. (9)
d   In her view, people with no legal right to be here, people who are filling American jobs, crowding American hospitals, lowering American wages during a brutal unemployment crisis, good people perhaps but not Americans, people violating our laws. For AOC, these people deserve aid, just like American

citizens, the ones who are hurting and out of work. [...] It was foolish to think that during our strongest period, our richest time, America could provide free everything to the rest of the world, but to demand the same thing when the economy is on the edge of collapse? When tens of millions of American citizens are in danger? That's not dumb, that's loathing for your own country, obviously. (10)

In the first excerpt, which comes from a "Your World" segment that discusses Ocasio-Cortez's reluctance to engage in a debate with conservative commentator Ben Shapiro, the Fox News host scales a two-person dispute up to a countrywide phenomenon. The Representative stands in, synecdochically, for "one side," presumably the Left, who is unwilling "to have civil debates," "to share ideas," and "to have the conversation" with the unmentioned opposition. Although the other imagined interlocutor in this conversation is presumably the Right, the host designates to "us" the meaning of all Americans when she states that Ocasio-Cortez's refusal to debate Shapiro contrasts "one of the things that has always made *us* great" and she poses the question "where does that leave *us* as a country?" (emphasis added). Thus, Ocasio-Cortez's behavior is at best indexed as disaligned with the "American way" and, at worst, is cast as ruinous for the country in that it undermines Americans' potential to "evolve" and "get better."

Excerpt b, from "Hannity," also designates dichotomic distinctions. The first dichotomy is constituted by renowned US presidents Reagan and FDR versus Ocasio-Cortez, and it is enacted most explicitly by calling her "the new radical extreme Socialist Democrat." The label "new" accentuates Ocasio-Cortez's inexperience compared to these two pillars of American history – which in itself threatens the Representative's historical coherence (Meade & Robles, 2017) – but the contrast between her and the former presidents is further and more poignantly underscored by the terms "radical" and "extreme," which evoke discourses of the threat of terrorism linked to Islam (e.g., "Islamic extremism" and "radical Muslims"; Wijsen, 2013) and present the highest degree of anti-Americanism in the post-9/11 era. Indexing Ocasio-Cortez as inexperienced and anti-American delegitimizes the Representative and achieves the effect of dismissing her claims.[3]

The second dichotomy Hannity constructs is "the American people" versus Ocasio-Cortez and "her government." Ocasio-Cortez is again cast as a threat – this time to the liberties and possessions of the

American people ("she wants you, the American people, to hand over the keys to your private businesses, your private property"). Reminiscent of Cold War-era anti-Communist propaganda, this invokes a future scenario in which Ocasio-Cortez plays the un-American lead who seizes the people's hard-earned belongings. Further reinforcing her un-Americanness, Hannity advances the conspiratorial notion that Ocasio-Cortez is not a member of and loyal to the US government but has "her" own government set against a producerism-driven definition of the "American people" (i.e., people who "create goods and services that make our lives easier and better"). The host elicits the populist narrative of "elites" versus "producing Americans" (Peck, 2019) by twice repeating that she "knows better" than "you," "we," and "the American people." Thus, Ocasio-Cortez's views are delegitimized because they are set against "the wisdom of common, productive folk" (Wells & Rochefort, 2021, p. 346).

In excerpt c, Tucker Carlson applies an ominous frame in his response to a police visit to the home of a podcaster who tweeted criticism of the Representative. Ocasio-Cortez is positioned as vastly powerful ("one of the largest political megaphones on earth" and "one of the most powerful politicians in America"), as power-hungry ("she wants more than that"), and aggressive (she "insists"). While the image of a politician who has already amassed vast power yet yearns for more is itself menacing, Carlson adds another superlative to the list by claiming that she is deploying "the most powerful companies in the world" for nefarious ends, or "to censor her political opponents." By suggesting that this behavior seems like "authoritarianism," or the antithesis of democracy, he chastises Ocasio-Cortez for acting in violation of American principles.

Lastly, in excerpt d, again from "Tucker Carlson Tonight," the host condemns Ocasio-Cortez's suggestion that undocumented immigrants receive relief funding, revealing strongly xenophobic and isolationist stances in the "us" versus "them" opposition he constructs between the American people and immigrants who are depriving Americans of jobs, healthcare services, and living wages, and are "violating our laws." Carlson depicts a harrowing and worsening scenario with emotionally charged language in which the American economy "is on the edge of collapse," and American citizens "are hurting," "out of work," and "in danger." By setting up this frightening backdrop, the host positions Ocasio-Cortez as a villain who is not only indifferent to the country's dire situation but she "loath[es]" her country.

I have argued that the primary delegitimization category evidenced in these four excerpts is mythopoesis, in which Ocasio-Cortez is depicted as the un- and/or anti-American antagonist of different doom scenarios. The arguments are constructed via the establishment of dichotomic distinctions, topoi of danger and threat, instancing conspiratorial beliefs, reference to right-wing populist ideologies, superlative constructions, and emotionally charged language. Ocasio-Cortez's "deviant" behaviors and activities "lead to unhappy endings" (van Leeuwen, 2008, p. 118), which are extreme and hyperbolic: they impede the evolution and betterment of the country, threaten the people's rights and liberties, undermine democracy, imperil the nation, and jeopardize the well-being of the American people.

However, the depiction of Ocasio-Cortez as anti-American and authoritarian is also strongly suggestive of her misuse, or even unethical use, of the authority with which she is vested as a government official. This attempt to cast doubt on the Representative's ability and suitability to govern will be the focus of the following section.

Undercutting authorization

Politicians are legitimized by their role as elected officials. According to van Leeuwen (2008), "legitimate authority is vested in people because of their status or role in a particular institution" (p. 106). This legitimate authority, however, can be called into question by undermining the authority, expertise, and credibility that elected officials accrue by their electoral win and institutional role (Reyes, 2011; van Leeuwen, 2007). One way in which this delegitimization can be enacted is by depicting leaders as bereft of the characteristics often associated with respected authorities, such as intelligence, rationality, acumen, preparation, and work ethic. The Fox News hosts under study, in fact, strove to portray Ocasio-Cortez as lacking these qualities chiefly by means of negative other-presentation, realized with the discursive strategies of nomination, predication, and ad hominem attacks.

One set of negatively connoted attributions used by Fox News hosts and their guests denotes Ocasio-Cortez's mental deficiency and intellectual incapacity. For instance, in segment 7, Barstool Sports founder Dave Portnoy states "and these morons who have no idea what we do jump into the fray like Alexandria Ocasio-Cortez, O-crazy-io," thereby using a simile to equate Ocasio-Cortez to "morons" and coining an insulting nickname for the Representative. Another example occurred in segment 10 in which Tucker Carlson uses a superlative to index her psychological incapacity: "Alexandria Ocasio-Cortez, the dumbest, most unhappy[4] member of Congress." These debasing nominations and evaluations deny Ocasio-Cortez's intellectual capacities and, therefore, call into question her ability to govern. Relatedly, the logic and clarity of the Representative's (often ideological) propositions is questioned by means of attributing to her the traits of irrationality (e.g., "You can't make it up. Is she really working for the [Republican National Council] secretly? Probably," segment 10), ignorance (e.g., "She obviously doesn't understand that capitalism is what allows us to flourish as a nation," segment 8), and unintelligibility (e.g., "What is she talking about?," segment 8).

Many of the negative predications expressed against Ocasio-Cortez debase her in terms of her unpreparedness (already referenced in excerpt b). In segment 8, host Jesse Watters and conservative pundit Tomi Lahren discuss a series of brief excerpts of different Ocasio-Cortez interviews framed as gaffes with the recurring chyron caption[5] "Socialist Stumble." In reference to Ocasio-Cortez's response to a question about Israeli–Palestinian relations, Lahren highlights her limited political experience: "As we know, she really doesn't have a lot of policy experience. This isn't her strong suit." Then, commenting on Ocasio-Cortez's assertions about unemployment, Lahren states: "She doesn't get it at all. But it just keeps getting better and better every time she opens her mouth. [...] It's always interesting to watch a train wreck." Together, these negative evaluations depict Ocasio-Cortez as not only inexperienced and unprepared[6] to assume the role of lawmaker but also as utterly disastrous. Watters replies to his guest: "Do you remember when I used to go out and do those street interviews and talk to people, they were totally clueless? She reminds me of a guest on Watters' World." Thus, Ocasio-Cortez is cast as a non-expert who is "totally clueless."[7] If, as maintained by Reyes (2011), "authoritative speech is a speech associated with authoritative people" who are more persuasive, heeded, and followed (pp. 786–787), then situating the lawmaker as being ill prepared and uninformed delegitimizes Ocasio-Cortez through the strategy of (lacking) authorization.

Reference to Ocasio-Cortez's youth is another way in which doubt is cast on her legitimate authority. Oftentimes, the Representative's age (group) is mentioned in passing, as when Jesse Watters introduces her as "socialist *millennial* Alexandria Ocasio-Cortez"

Attacks on a progressive newcomer 73

(segment 8) at the start of his segment, but with a very precise intent. Age can become negative other-presentation when it occurs within politics, a domain in which (political) experience has traditionally been the cornerstone for success. Being called young can, therefore, be a covert way to delegitimize a lawmaker.

e   At the age of 31, she is a much sought-after voice on every possible topic from economics to the way society is designed to the details of complex foreign policy questions. (segment 9)
f   If [you...] realized that actually some unmarried 29-year-old member of Congress probably should be in charge of your childbearing decisions [...] (1)

In excerpts e and f, both spoken by Tucker Carlson, her age cited in numbers has a more manifest effect. In the former, her young age is set against the extreme case formulations "much sought-after" and "every possible topic" to mock both Ocasio-Cortez and those who attend to her opinions on important issues. In the latter, which is an excerpt from a segment intended to achieve a parodical effect further discussed later in the chapter (see example 2), her age follows her marital status with the aim of emphasizing that this Congressperson should not "be in charge of your childbearing decisions." Yet, while the link between Ocasio-Cortez's institutional role and Americans' childbearing decisions may be more straightforward for some,[8] reference to her marital status is more insinuating. This status is drawn on as a resource to question her moral judgment and situate her as in defiance of family values and in discord with underlying right-wing populist gendered ideology which favors women in traditional gender roles (Wodak, 2015).

Another way in which Fox News cast doubt on Ocasio-Cortez's authority, expertise, and credibility is by attacking her integrity, which delegitimizes her as a lawmaker since truth and honesty are highly desired qualities of a leader (Ross & Rivers, 2017). This delegitimization strategy was employed by Fox News hosts by accusing Ocasio-Cortez of presenting a misleading self-portrayal, manipulating the truth, and employing fallacious argumentation strategies. One such instance can be found in Ben Shapiro's comment about Ocasio-Cortez's statement to the audience of a Hanukkah event that she has Jewish ancestors delivered on "Fox News @ Night": "I mean I'm very sick of politicians just generally claiming that some sort of heritage allows them to get off the hook for their current political position" (segment 3). This reply positions Ocasio-Cortez amongst other dishonest politicians who connive to evade public scrutiny over their policies.

Another way in which Ocasio-Cortez manipulates the American people, in the words of Fox News hosts, is by making (allegedly) false accusations of sexism and misogyny. We see this unfold in segments 4 and 5. In segment 4, Ben Shapiro responds to the Representative's tweet where she equated his "unsolicited" request for a debate to "catcalling" and says she "invoke[s] victim status" and "play[s] the 'I'm a female and therefore I'm being victimized'" card – which "rallies the base" and gets "folks in the media [...] very excited" – to avoid "a discussion with somebody who asks her tough questions." In segment 5, Republican Gubernatorial candidate Ron DeSantis responds to Ocasio-Cortez's indignation after he called her "this girl Ocasio-Cortez or whatever she is" and declares she "tr[ies] to play identity politics" to "obscure scrutiny on her views which are socialist and they're wrapped in ignorance" (5). Thus, both Shapiro and DeSantis allege that Ocasio-Cortez – helped by Democrats and the media – fakes her indignation and manipulates the narrative to avoid engaging in a debate and to conceal critique of her policies. Since great effort is made by politicians to be credible, attacks on the veracity of her outrage undermine the Representative's trustworthiness, another essential quality of a leader.

The charge that she "invoke[s] victim status" and "tr[ies] to play" a part to gain an advantage conveys the notion that she is misleading the people by presenting herself as vulnerable. In a similar vein, Tucker Carlson frames Ocasio-Cortez as a wolf in sheep's clothing:

g Alexandria Ocasio-Cortez isn't a power mad demagogue. No no. She's a vulnerable young woman just trying to protect herself from assault. To disagree with her is to injure her. (9)

In this excerpt, Carlson casts doubt on the sincerity of the image she (allegedly) projects as "a vulnerable young woman" and her discontent with those who attack her. He further dismisses claims, also echoed in other top ten Fox News videos,[9] that there is more to criticism of Ocasio-Cortez that meets the eye. Furthermore, his mocking tone suggests that Ocasio-Cortez *is* actually "a power mad demagogue." This is consistent with other attacks, already mentioned earlier, of the Representative's authoritarianism. It also gives credence to the notion that Ocasio-Cortez heads the Democratic party, which was suggested in both segments 5 ("The chairman of the whole [Democratic] party said that she is the wave of the future") and segment 6 ("The person that's really leading the Democratic party, Ocasio-Cortez").

Considering the insinuation that Ocasio-Cortez leads her party, it is curious that another attack on Ocasio-Cortez takes the form of framing her as a puppet. Jesse Watters stated twice, in segments 2 and 8, that Ocasio-Cortez is "all sizzle and no steak," suggesting that she fails to measure up to the hype. In segment 2, he provides a meticulous account of Ocasio-Cortez's "rise to the top," which was no "accident," by design and commandeered by other (notably male) masterminds. He describes her ascent as follows:

h She was a planned, packaged, and processed candidate sold to a hungry young generation by a slick and shallow media. Empty calories Cortez. Her story begins with Bernie Sanders. His failed run for the presidency in 2016. Where a campaign volunteer in Silicon Valley and executive Saikat Chakrabarti began recruiting hundreds of progressives for house races. Chakrabarti identified AOC and after realizing his product's potential, he decided he would run her campaign. He cast her, she won, and then he named himself her chief of staff. So, it is safe to say that with Chakrabarti writing the script AOC was making noise on the left. He was the brains behind the Green New Deal. Not AOC. (segment 2)

By insinuating that "her story" was started by Bernie Sanders, was promoted by "a slick and shallow media," and was orchestrated by political advisor Saikat Chakrabarti, Watters removes Ocasio-Cortez from the helm of her own political career. In so doing, he tarnishes the existential coherence of her carefully crafted "bootstrap" narrative,[10] and the fact that she was "cast" frames her as an inauthentic performer. The lawmaker's ascent and success are carefully attributed to a third party: "he cast her," is in charge (he "[wrote] the script"), made all the decisions (he not only ran her campaign but "decided he would"), and "was the brains behind" even her most noteworthy piece of legislation, the Green New Deal. Watters concludes by stating: "So it is safe to say that with Chakrabarti writing the script AOC was making noise on the left," where the impersonal construction "it is safe to say" serves as an intensification strategy that conveys greater epistemic certainty and the sentence-initial position of the prepositional phrase "with Chakrabarti writing the script" ensures that attribution for Ocasio-Cortez's notoriety is assigned to the third party.

Within this narration, Watters reinforces the notion that Ocasio-Cortez lacks agency with dehumanizing metaphors. He calls her "empty calories Cortez," echoing his introductory bit on the unsuccessful marketing strategies of a failed Coca Cola product. In addition to objectifying the Representative, this label debases the lawmaker by positioning her as unsubstantial, undesirable, and damaging, akin to nutrient–poor foods or beverages. He also commodifies Ocasio-Cortez and represents her as "packaged and processed" and "sold to a hungry young generation" before explicitly naming her a "product." This representation of the lawmaker as a carefully curated commodity frames her as inauthentic and fraudulent, and contradicts the image she built of herself as an ordinary American who was driven to pursue politics to fight for the people. Furthermore, a US Representative being engineered by a third party whose intentions are unknown reads as nefarious. In fact, the description of Chakrabarti's role evokes the conspiratorial belief that "there is a secret master who pulls the strings behind the scene of those who are officially in power" (Fuchs, 2021, p. 118). This conspiracy theory has the effect of situating Ocasio-Cortez as a pawn who has no agency and is acting on behalf of others, and as deceitful since she is not the authentic politician in the political "rags-to-riches" tale she told.

Watters brings this contradiction to the foreground at the end of segment 2, when he states:

i   In fact, did AOC run for Congress just to be famous? She is on the red carpet more than Ryan Seacrest. Ocasio-Cortez says she represents the downtrodden of society. But has she actually done anything for her constituents? (2)

He labels her motivations for running for office as not only suspect and in opposition to her claim to represent "the downtrodden of society" but to be famous, as suggested by her frequent presence on the red carpet – "more than" American media personality Ryan Seacrest. This can be seen as "position-based" authorization in that the position as elected official is an opportunity for self-aggrandizing narcissism (i.e., an inappropriate use of authority) (Ross & Rivers, 2017; Vaara, 2014). Lastly, with the rhetorical question, Watters suggests that Ocasio-Cortez has *not* "actually done anything for her constituents," challenging her legitimacy to her institutional role authority because she is not accomplishing the work that is expected of her. The host's question also suggests that

Ocasio-Cortez is idle and futile, so her behavior runs contrary to the producerist ideal.

Across the ten segments under study, Fox News coverage of Representative Ocasio-Cortez attempted to undermine the personal, expert, and role model authority she accrued as an elected official because of her mental deficiency, unpreparedness, youth, unmarried status, dishonesty, fraudulent nature, and inauthenticity. These assigned attributes perpetuated the notion that she was unprepared, unfit, and unsuited for office. By doing so, these pundits attempted to convince the audience that the Representative, who was neither competent nor qualified, should be neither respected nor revered, and therefore her standpoint should be dismissed.

Much of this work to delegitimize the Representative was done by selecting decontextualized excerpts of her speeches and interviews and commenting about them on Fox News. This recontextualization process became one of the most powerful mechanisms through which network hosts negatively evaluated the Representative. For this reason, the next section homes in on one of the Fox News segments to examine this process in more detail.

The recontextualization of Ocasio-Cortez's words onto Fox News

This section zeroes in on the most viewed excerpt of the ten videos: the 20 March 2019 "Tucker Carlson Tonight" (henceforth *TCT*) segment entitled "Ocasio-Cortez lashes out at unflattering likability poll" to examine how Representative Ocasio-Cortez's original words were reframed and filtered in their recontextualization onto a Fox News show.

The *TCT* segment under study begins with host Tucker Carlson citing a poll that suggested more New Yorkers disliked than liked the Representative, and her Twitter response to these results. Ocasio-Cortez's original tweet, shown as original quotation (1), posted on 18 January 2019 was a reply to a tweet authored by David Atkins, which read: "It's interesting to see centrists suddenly downplay or ignore the effects of racism, sexism and Fox News targeting when discussing @AOC's overall approval ratings."

1 *Original quotation* – Alexandria Ocasio-Cortez (AOC): When "centrists" care more about the GOP base than the Dem base, bigotry gets legitimized. This is *the* playbook. GOP does it w/ virtually every Dem figure who isn't a white male: otherize,

demonize + splinter. It's vital that we adapt & dismantle this approach, not cow to it.

Recontextualization on TCT – Tucker Carlson (TC): [brows furrowed] How did someone who's been in Congress only a few months turn off so many people and so quickly? The Congresswoman has a ready answer for that as she does for most things. As she explained on Twitter, Republicans working in concert with that dastardly Fox News [adopts second-party voice], quote, otherize and [smirks, raises eyebrows] demonize anyone who isn't, quote, a white male. In other words, it's bigotry pure and simple. Those may look like bad poll numbers, what they really are is racism. Now, it's possible you will scoff at this explanation. It is whiny and predictable and totally self-serving. It's also unsupported by evidence.

A comparison of the contents of Ocasio-Cortez's tweet and its recontextualization on *TCT* reveals similarities: both refer to a system of (legitimization of) bigotry by Republicans that targets non-white, non-male Democrats. However, there are important changes in terms of the recontextualization principles of additions, presence, and abstraction (Fairclough, 2003). Carlson's facial expressions are additions that serve as visual cues to negative evaluations: his furrowed brows transmit skeptical disdain, his second-party voice mocks, and his smirk and raised eyebrows cast doubt on the seriousness of the accusations. Then, while sexism – included in both Atkins' tweet and inherent in the genderonym "male" – is backgrounded in Carlson's response (where racism is explicitly stated), the host's commentary is imbued with gendered language. He suggests that the Representative talks too much, a trait attributed to women more so than to men, and in the evaluation of the tweet, Carlson uses the term "whiny," a pejorative adjective associated with the dangerous talk of women seldom applied to men (Ferguson, 2000). By directly citing only selected words and presenting the tweet with negative evaluations, the *TCT* host reframes the original quotation: a call to action to dismantle a racist and sexist system becomes a "whiny," "predictable," "totally self-serving," and "unsupported" excuse.

Subsequent to this introduction, Carlson presents what he calls a "litmus test" for the souls of his viewers. What ensues is a game-like exercise in which the host asks his viewers whether they agree with Ocasio-Cortez's opinions within a series of brief aired excerpts of interviews and posts with the aim of demonstrating the absurdity of her views and creating a parodical effect. The first is a clip of a video Ocasio-Cortez posted on her Instagram account on 24 February

2019 (2), which begins with a conditional sentence in which a bleak image of the future – or planetary disaster – is projected to skew the opinion of viewers in favor of reform. By employing this linguistic structure and citing ominous consequences, the Representative uses the strategy of legitimization through mythopoesis to appeal to viewers' emotions, justify immediate action, and ultimately legitimize her proposed legislation, namely, the Green New Deal.

2 *Original quotation* - AOC: Our planet is going to be a disaster if we don't turn this ship around and so it's basically like there's scientific consensus that the lives of children are gonna be very difficult and it <u>does lead</u> – I think – young people to (.) have a legitimate question, you know, should- (.) is it okay to still have children?

Recontextualization on TCT - TC: First we're gonna consider AOC's views on children. She doesn't have any and there's a reason for that: [brows furrowed] she cares too much. [brows raised] Her heart is too big. Watch her explain:

[video excerpt aired]

TC: [brows furrowed] Is it okay to still have children? That is AOC's question to you. Now if you answered: 'are you kidding? Of course it's okay to have children. And, by the way, back off you authoritarian creep. How many kids I have is none of your business.'

In spite of, and arguably because of, this excerpt's aims, no mention of climate change transpires in its recontextualization on *TCT*. This omission is likely ideologically and/or politically grounded because both right-wing populist parties and their supporters (Lockwood, 2018) and American conservatives and Republicans (McCright & Dunlap, 2011) are more likely to be climate skeptics and hostile toward climate change policy. Instead, the introduction to the video redefines the topic to the Representative's "views on children." By specifying that the Representative "doesn't have any" children, Carlson adds personal information missing in the original quotation and denies her the "female advantage" on child-care and children's issues held by female politicians who are mothers (Stalsburg, 2010). Then, the original question, preceded by the mitigating "I think," the hedge "you know" and the self-initiated repair, is reframed from a rhetorical device to a directed question to the *TCT* audience. The omission of references to climate change legislation and the literal interpretation of her question presents a misleading picture of Ocasio-Cortez's standpoint, or a "straw man fallacy" – which "amounts to 'twisting

80 *Attacks on a progressive newcomer*

somebody's words', that is to say, to presenting a distorted picture of the antagonist's standpoint in order to be able to refute the standpoint or argument more easily and to make it less tenable" (Reisigl & Wodak, 2001, p. 73). This provides Carlson with the opportunity to make her standpoint less tenable and to position Ocasio-Cortez as an authoritarian menace to individual freedom.

The third quotation is an excerpt of an 8 January 2019 MSNBC interview with Rachel Maddow:

3   *Original quotation* - AOC: Those women and children trying to come here with nothing but the shirts on their back to <u>create</u> an opportunity and to p- <u>provide</u> for this nation are acting more in the American tradition [nodding] than this President is right now.

Recontextualization on TCT - TC: This one's about immigration:

[video excerpt aired]

TC: So the question is: [brows furrowed] 'who is more American? [eyebrows raised] <u>Actual</u> Americans or <u>foreigners</u> who spit on our customs and mock our laws by sneaking into our country illegally and calling us racist if we try to make them leave?'

Both the original quotation and its recontextualization describe immigrants and create dichotomies, but they are pointedly distinct: "immigrants" versus "this President" in the former, and "actual Americans" versus "foreigners" in the latter. While the use of "actual Americans" – rearranged as first, and more prominent, of the two elements in Carlson's rendition – to stand in for "this President" may be interpreted as a metonymical extension, this shift also injects Ocasio-Cortez's utterance with a new anti-American meaning. Moreover, Ocasio-Cortez's statement, an emotional appeal to the plight of immigrants, is characterized by moves of positive other-presentation indicative of anti-racist ideological talk while in its recontextualization on *TCT* it is reframed within the mental models prejudiced people have about immigrants and employs negative other-presentation strategies (van Dijk, 2000). Immigrants are described via predicational identification in terms of negative prejudiced criminalization ("mock our laws," "sneaking into our country illegally"), incivility ("spit on our customs"), and bigotry ("calling us racist"). The Representative and Carlson use similar argumentation moves and appeal to the viewers' emotions by "starkly emphasising the situation of those they speak for" (van Dijk, 2000,

p. 111), but the former seeks sympathy for immigrants, while the latter solicits protection of "our" customs, laws, and integrity.

The fourth and final recontextualized quotation under study, the last excerpt aired in the segment, was from an interview with Anderson Cooper (AC) that aired on "60 Minutes" in January 2019:

4   *Original quotation* – AC: One of the criticisms of you is that— that your math is fuzzy. The Washington Post recently awarded you four Pinocchios— […]

AOC: I think that there's a lot of people more concerned about being <u>precisely factually</u> and <u>semantically</u> correct than about being <u>morally</u> right.

Recontextualization on TCT – TC: And now for the final question on our test. This one is the daily double. See how you do.

[video excerpt aired]

'factually correct' [smirks]. Now this question gets right to the heart of it all: [brows furrowed] are you one of those troglodytes who still cares about [eyebrows raised] <u>facts</u>? [brows furrowed] About <u>numbers</u> and <u>evidence</u> and physical reality? It's 2019, man, physics is just a preference. [eyebrows raised] If you persist in being <u>factually</u> correct and continue to read books [air quotes] and speak in complete sentences [air quotes], please know that you are committing racism.

This final example is particularly compelling for several reasons. Carlson mocks Ocasio-Cortez for dismissing factual and semantic accuracy in favor of moral righteousness and applies a jocular frame when he exaggerates her claims by citing "numbers and evidence," "physics," "read[ing] books," and "speak[ing] in complete sentences." He further makes an illogical link to racism, which both reinforces the claim that Ocasio-Cortez is irrational and situates the accusation of racism as hackneyed and meaningless. Yet, there is also a sense of irony that transpires from Carlson's critique. In the original quotation, Ocasio-Cortez minimizes facts and precision over intuition, which is exactly one of the aspects that Peck (2021) identified in the cultural populism of Fox News, where outrage trumps expertise, credentials, and empirical evidence. Its reference to moral righteousness is also strongly evocative of the moral superiority of "the people" in populist rhetoric (Kazin, 2017).

Bauman and Briggs (1990) argued that "to decontextualize and recontextualize a text" is "an act of control" (p. 76). Indeed, as fragments of Ocasio-Cortez's discourse were moved from their original context into the *TCT* context, elements of the original text were rearranged and abstracted, included and excluded, and foregrounded and backgrounded. These manipulations of the original text either reframed or outright omitted Ocasio Cortez's underlying anti-administration, environmentalist, and anti-racist ideologies. The recontextualization process delegitimized Ocasio-Cortez's words, arguments, and policies, principally by using debasing personal attributions but also by building a "straw man fallacy" (Reisigl & Wodak, 2001). In so doing, it served to position the Representative as whiny, authoritarian, and anti-American, and also to completely rewrite and/or discredit her message. Yet, analysis of this process also evidenced some interesting commonalities between the discourses of Ocasio-Cortez and Fox News hosts, such as emotionally charged language, mythopoesis, and affinity with lay epistemic culture.

Fox News coverage of Alexandria Ocasio-Cortez

Thus far, the present chapter has detailed the mechanisms by which Fox News strove to delegitimize Ocasio-Cortez, and furthered understandings of how strategies of (de)legitimization, traditionally focused on institutions, apply to individuals (Ross & Rivers, 2017). A series of running threads were recognized within Fox News coverage of the Representative. First, Fox News hosts used emotional, stirring language to alert the audience of the threat posed by the Representative and her actions to American ideals and the wellbeing of the American people. Then, they used negative references and predications – including name-calling – to cast doubt on her intelligence, rationality, and acumen, and they called attention to her age, inexperience, and marital status to portray her as ill prepared and a non-expert. Next, the narrative of her political rise was rewritten to frame another person – not least a male – as the protagonist of her story with the effect of designating her as a pawn and a fraud, and of threatening her credibility and the coherence of the personal narrative and political self that Ocasio-Cortez so painstakingly crafted during her first campaign.

The challenge to Ocasio-Cortez's legitimacy centered on her identity to a much higher degree than the tenuousness of her policies and proposed legislation. This often played out in the linguistic form of fallacious *argumentum ad hominem* – "a verbal attack on the antagonist's personality and character (of her or his credibility, integrity, honesty, expertise, competence and so on) instead of argumentatively trying to refute the antagonist's arguments"

(Reisigl & Wodak, 2001, p. 72). The impulse to resort to a slew of personal attacks over logical argumentation resulted in paradoxical representations of the Representative: on the one hand, she was a conniving mastermind and the leader of the Democratic party, and on the other hand, she was a clueless puppet; on the one hand, she was young, inexperienced, and unprepared, and on the other hand, her actions were perfectly aligned with the longstanding tradition of (opposition) politicians who manipulate the truth and instrumentalize victimhood.

Another fallacious argumentation scheme utilized in the analyzed segments was the "straw man" fallacy, which emerged most palpably in the analysis of the recontextualization mechanisms in the top video. In the *TCT* segment, host Tucker Carlson manipulated and simplified Ocasio-Cortez's message when he reinserted it within his show. Through this recontextualization, Carlson provided "a sort of 'preferred reading' for the discourse" that created a new act of communication often with characteristics that diverged strongly from the original act (Blommaert, 2020, p. 398) and contained Carlson's own ideological aims. The new, transformed message reverberated echoes of populist discourses.

All of the segments were, in fact, imbued with right-wing populist references and sentiments. Fox News hosts constructed "us" versus "them" dichotomies characteristic of populist discourse, such as "the people" versus "immigrants" in segments 1 and 10, and "the people" versus "Ocasio-Cortez and her government" in segment 6. In the former, it is implied that "the people" are white and of European heritage, while in the latter, Hannity explicitly defined "the people" according to the producerist ideal of those who "create goods and services." The former association both feeds into xenophobic ideologies and values and insinuates that Ocasio-Cortez's pro-immigrant stance is anti-American (see example 3). The latter not only elicits anti-elite sentiment that positions Ocasio-Cortez as unproductive (also evidenced in segment 2), but reference to "her government" also invokes the conspiratorial notion of a powerful, hidden cabal advanced by groups such as QAnon. This is not the only time conspiratorial beliefs are instanced: the media, a frequent populist antagonist that is depicted as biased, "slick and shallow" (segment 2), are represented as colluding with other parties (i.e., Sanders and Chakrabarti) to mastermind and advance the Representative's career.

One aspect that has not thus far been addressed is the additional insights that transpire when this coverage was posted online. A first interpretative frame was already applied when the Fox News segments were given their titles on YouTube (see Table 5.1). In these titles, Ocasio-Cortez "lashes out" at a poll, falsely "claim[s]" a heritage, and "bashes capitalism," which imply an extreme emotional response to criticism, deceitfulness and appropriation, and the demolition of key American values, respectively. The language that is instead used to describe what hosts and pundits do within the videos suggests verbally and physically battering the Representative, as they "[sound] off," "[hit]," and "[shred]." However, the comment feature of YouTube provides access not only to other evaluations of the Representative, but it functioned as a space in which commenters negotiated, re-oriented, and re-entextualized the messages and language contained in the videos. Thus, the final section of this chapter explores the YouTube comments to the most viewed video to investigate users' comments to Fox News coverage of Ocasio-Cortez on the social media platform.

YouTube comments about Fox News coverage

The analysis of the 20,467 YouTube user comments to the *TCT* segment "Ocasio-Cortez lashes out at unflattering likability poll" began with keyness analysis, used to understand "the main concepts, topics or attitudes discussed in a text or corpus" (Gabrielatos, 2018, p. 225).

Table 5.2, which displays the top 30 keywords,[12] shows the predictable presence of a series of abbreviations and shortenings

Table 5.2 Results of the comparative keyword analysis

	Item	Freq	Keyness		Item	Freq	Keyness
1	Fart[11]	410	398.134	16	Procreate	53	83.551
2	Hamburger	401	216.185	17	Stupid	995	80.158
3	Bartender	258	178.992	18	Unlikable	41	77.709
4	Moron	376	155.461	19	Twat	40	77.071
5	Factually	140	142.673	20	Morally	195	72.95
6	Idiot	952	132.564	21	Commie	70	69.087
7	Lmao	140	132.478	22	Cow	482	66.494
8	Dumb	646	129.928	23	Maga	54	65.869
9	Dumbass	84	123.283	24	Bimbo	48	63.189
10	Bigot	185	116.509	25	Lmfao	34	60.699
11	Racist	1,165	115.749	26	Smh	35	60.256
12	Bartending	55	106.381	27	Dingbat	29	59.005
13	Pirro	133	95.75	28	Uneducated	58	56.377
14	Twit	59	89.839	29	Lol	642	55.56
15	Stupidity	165	89.22	30	Kotex	26	54.878

typical of online discourse. The first set, or "lmao," "lmfao," and "lol," are acronyms and initialisms that express laughter and serve to mock, while "smh," or shaking my head, expresses disapproval. The clipping and diminutive "commie" stands for communist.

One-third of the keywords from the YouTube comment corpus denote Ocasio-Cortez's mental deficiency and intellectual incapacity: "moron," "idiot," "dumb," "dumbass," "twit," "stupidity," "stupid," "bimbo," "dingbat," and "uneducated." Interestingly, many of these terms were used with reference to the Representative by other Fox News hosts and guests in the top viewed videos (e.g., "moron," "idiot," "dumb"), but not in the specific video on which the users were commenting. This may be suggestive of the tendency for users to take up the language used across Fox News segments dedicated to Ocasio-Cortez in their comments. Noteworthy is the presence of the term "bimbo," which, alongside "twat" and "kotex," the feminine product brand used by commenters to stand in for "Cortez," serve as gender-based and sexist epithets. These keywords indicate that commenters resorted to ad hominem attacks against Ocasio-Cortez instead of trying to refute her arguments (Reisigl & Wodak, 2001), the same strategy frequently employed by Fox News hosts, anchors, and guests.

The Sketch Engine concordance tool was used to see how the terms "bartender" and "bartending" were used in context. This revealed that commenters used these terms within appeals for the Representative to return to her previous employment (e.g., "Go back to *bartending* – you probably sucked at that too;" "Make AOC a *bartender* again," which was also represented by the acronym MABA, a play on Trump's slogan MAGA) or to point to her inexperience (e.g., "Its hard to not make fun of aoc, when she uses *bartending* school as her basis for everything she's learned [sic];" "This is what you get when you put a *bartender* in charge of important matters"). Reference to Ocasio-Cortez's inexperience emerged as a salient category in the delegitimization of the Representative across segments, and within the *TCT* segment to which the commenters were replying, which is indicative of alignment with the network's evaluation.

There were also 133 occurrences of the last name "Pirro." When the *TCT* video was posted on YouTube, Jeanine Pirro, at the time host of the Fox News show "Justice with Judge Jeanine Pirro", had been recently suspended for anti-Muslim remarks against Representative Ilhan Omar. Her suspension went on to last only two weeks. The frequent use of her name in response to a news segment that did not at all reference Pirro suggests that the YouTube comment section to this *TCT* video served as an intimate, digital space in which Fox News viewers aired their network-specific grievances. It also is suggestive of the link that commenters made between the content of the *TCT* segment – and particularly reference to Ocasio-Cortez as a "racist" against whites and a "bigot" – and anti-Muslim sentiment.

The next analytical step comprised the analysis of comments gathered from a randomly generated sample of five concordance lines containing the most frequent 3–4-gram of the YouTube comment corpus, or "she is a:"

1 *SHE IS A* HIRED ACTOR- LOOK IT UP PEOPLE!!!
2 *She is a* verifiable lunatic, useless, a liability and a danger to herself and democracy at large.
3 Watch AOC eyes move, *she is a* born liar and racist
4 *She is a* true Wacko.. No faith in God whatsoever. So immature, no life experience..she's laughable. Who would take anything she says seriously???
5 The only way I can describe this woman is this way, *she is a* total stupid socialist and unfit for any office other than the drive up window at Jack in the Box, W[e]ndy's or Burger King.

These comments, like many YouTube comments, are brief and incisive, and they all contain negative predications. In example (1), in which the use of capitalization and three consecutive exclamation marks suggest increased volume (screaming), Ocasio-Cortez is characterized as "a hired actor," and therefore inauthentic and as a pawn. This is reminiscent of Jesse Watters' narrative reconstruction of the Representative's political career as orchestrated by third parties. Other negative characterizations occur across examples. She is depicted as: mentally unstable in examples (2) ("lunatic") and (4) ("Wacko"); deceitful in example (3) ("she is a born liar"); unfit for Congress in examples (4) ("immature, no life experience") and (5) ("unfit for any office other than the drive up window"); irreligious in example (4) ("No faith in God whatsoever"); a perpetrator of "reverse racism" in example (3) ("she is a [...] racist"); and as a threat to democracy in example (2) ("a danger to [...] democracy at large"). In all, the comments are teeming with personal attacks that strive to refute Ocasio-Cortez's legitimacy as an elected official.

The original content of the most viewed Fox News segment that featured coverage of Ocasio-Cortez on YouTube underwent a transformative process when it was recontextualized and re-entextualized within user comments. These comments included features we would expect from this transformation such as markers of informal, online talk. There is also evidence that commenters scaled up the Representative-focused content on *TCT*. First, users increased the intensity of their offensive remarks toward Ocasio-Cortez with misogynist terms, certainly a byproduct of the anonymity afforded by the social media platform, that rendered explicit the sexist stereotypes that were implicit within Fox News coverage (such as those related to marital and parental status, and traditional gender roles). Second, commenters were able to make appeals to and circulate wider right-wing populist, nationalist, racist, xenophobic, and Islamophobic ideologies – occasioned by the use of "Pirro," "racist," "commie," and reference to MAGA. The vitriolic and ideological nature of these users' responses to this *TCT* segment suggests that the YouTube comment section of a video posted by the official Fox News account serves as a space where exclusionary and discriminatory ideologies are reinforced and thrive (Perrino, 2017).

Notes

1 Roughly one third of the comments were written within a week after the video was posted.
2 A token is the smallest unit that a corpus consists of, and it normally refers to a word form, punctuation, digit, abbreviations and anything else that occurs between spaces.
3 Accusations that the left overapplies the label 'racist' is a frequent motif on Fox News. In the same segment, Hannity states: "Like any far-left extremist, the lawmaker's views would not be complete without everyone thinking everyone pretty much is a racist." These charges trivialize racism by suggesting that it is a groundless, hackneyed justification excessively used by (left-leaning) politicians.
4 Carlson's label of Ocasio-Cortez as 'the most unhappy' member of Congress is indicative of another frequent conservative critique of the Left as persistently dissatisfied and pessimistic.
5 Lower thirds or chyrons are graphic elements that appears in the lower area of the screen of a news broadcast with concise statements that highlight/summarize the news story presented.
6 This emphasis on her lack of preparation was echoed in other segments as well. For instance, Ben Shapiro stated in segment 4: "I don't think she has the information or the philosophy at her disposal to actually answer [tough] questions well and she knows that."
7 This debasing attribution is also used by Dave Portnoy in segment 7 who states: "Again, I don't think she has any clue who we are or what we do. She jumped in the fray like an idiot."

88 *Attacks on a progressive newcomer*

8 It is ironic that a Fox News Host criticizes a member of Congress for meddling with childbearing decisions when the network has advocated pro-life legislation.
9 For instance, Ben Shapiro says: "the usual line is that 'If you criticize Ocasio-Cortez in any way this is because you are obsessed with Ocasio-Cortez'" (segment 3), and Jesse Watters states: "Because AOC thinks if you criticize her, it just means you really want to date her" (segment 2).
10 The Representative's 'rags-to-riches'-like story of bartender/waitress turned Congresswoman is occasioned by Carlson in segment 9 to frame her as impressive, powerful, and threatening.
11 The words with the highest keyness, or 'fart' and 'hamburger', referred to the content one of the interviews discussed in the TCT segment that referred to 'cow farts' in terms of the environmental impact of animals' methane emissions. This segment was not included in the previous section due to space constraints.
12 According to Scott (1998), "a word is said to be 'key' if […] its frequency in the text when compared with its frequency in a reference corpus is such that the statistical probability as computed by an appropriate procedure is smaller than or equal to a p-value specified by the user" (p. 71).

References

Bauman, R. & Briggs C.L. (1990). Poetics and performances as critical perspectives on language and social life. *Annual Review of Anthropology,* 19, 59–88.
Blommaert, J. (2020). Political discourse in post-digital societies. *Trabalhos em Linguistica Aplicada,* 59(1), 390–403.
Blommaert, J. (2005). *Discourse.* Cambridge: Cambridge University Press.
Fairclough, N. (2003). *Analyzing Discourse: Textual Analysis for Social Research.* London: Routledge.
Ferguson, K.E. (2000). Elements of a feminist discourse. In Warwick Organizational Behaviour Staff (Eds.). *Organizational Studies: Critical Perspectives on Business and Management* (pp. 950–1000). London: Routledge.
Fuchs C. (2021). *Communicating COVID-19.* Bingley: Emerald Publishing Limited.
Gabrielatos, C. (2018). Keyness analysis: Nature, metrics and techniques. In C. Taylor & A. Marchi (Eds.). *Corpus Approaches to Discourse* (pp. 225–258). London-New York: Routledge.
Jakubíček, M., et al. (2013). The TenTen Corpus Family. In 7th International Corpus Linguistics Conference CL. 125–127.
Kazin, M. (2017). *The Populist Persuasion: An American History.* Ithaca-London: Cornell University Press.

Lillis, M. (2020). 'Ocasio-Cortez accosted by GOP lawmaker over remarks', *The Hill*, Retrieved from: https://thehill.com/homenews/house/508259-ocaasio-cortez-accosted-by-gop-lawmaker-over-remarks-that-kind-of

Lockwood, M. (2018). Right-wing populism and the climate change agenda: Exploring the linkages. *Environmental Politics*, 27(4), 712–732.

McCright, A.M. & Dunlap, R.E. (2011). The politicization of climate change and polarization in the American public's views of global warming, 2001–2010. *The Sociological Quarterly*, 52, 155–194.

Meade, M. & Robles, J. (2017). Historical and existential coherence in political commercials. *Discourse & Communication*, 11(4), 404–432.

Peck, R. (2021). 'Listen to your gut': How Fox News's populist style changed the American public sphere and journalistic truth in the process. In H. Tumber & S. Waisbord (Eds.), *The Routledge Companion to Media Disinformation and Populism* (pp. 160–168). London-New York: Routledge.

Peck, R. (2019). *Fox Populism: Branding Conservatism as Working Class.* Cambridge: Cambridge University Press.

Perrino, S. (2017). Recontextualizing racialized stories on YouTube. *Narrative Inquiry*, 27(2), 261–285.

Reisigl, M. & Wodak, R. (2009). The discourse-historical approach (DHA). In R. Wodak & M. Meyer (Eds.), *Methods for Critical Discourse Analysis* (pp. 87–121). London: SAGE.

Reisigl, M. & Wodak, R. (2001). *Discourse and Discrimination: Rhetorics of Racism and Antisemitism.* London: Routledge.

Reyes, A. (2011). Strategies of legitimization in political discourse: From words to actions. *Discourse & Society*, 22(6), 781–807.

Ross, A.S. & Rivers, D.J. (2017). Digital cultures of political participation. *Discourse, Context and Media*, 16, 1–11.

Scott, M. (1998). *WordSmith Tools Manual, Version 3.0.* Oxford: Oxford University Press.

Skidmore, M.J. (2015). Populism and its perils: Language and politics. *Annales Universitatis Mariae Curie-Skłodowska Lublin*, 22(1), 7–22.

Stalsburg, B.L. (2010). Voting for mom: The political consequences of being a parent for male and female candidates. *Politics & Gender*, 6, 373–404.

Vaara, E. (2014). Struggles over legitimacy in the Eurozone crisis: Discursive legitimation strategies and their ideological underpinnings. *Discourse & Society*, 25(4), 500–518.

van Dijk, T.A. (2000). Ideologies, racism, and discourse. In J. ter Wal & M. Verkuyten (Eds.), *Comparative Perspectives on Racism* (pp. 91–116). Farnham: Ashgate.

van Leeuwen, T. (2008). *Discourse and Practice.* Oxford: Oxford University Press.

van Leeuwen, T. (2007). Legitimation in discourse and communication. *Discourse & Communication*, 1(1), 91–112.

Wells, C. & Rochefort, A. (2021). Populism and misinformation from the American revolution to the Twenty-First-Century United States. In H.

Tumber & S. Waisbord (Eds.), *The Routledge Companion to Media Disinformation and Populism* (pp. 345–355). London-New York: Routledge.

Wijsen, F. (2013). 'There are radical Muslims and normal Muslims': An analysis of the discourse on Islamic extremism. *Religion,* 43(1), 70–88.

Wodak, R. (2015). *The Politics of Fear.* Los Angeles: SAGE.

6 "Get used to me slaying"
The discursive realization of a "clapback queen"

Introduction

In September 2018, critics charged that the expensive wardrobe worn at a photoshoot by Alexandria Ocasio-Cortez, at the time the Democratic candidate for the NY-14 House seat, cast doubt on the authenticity of her self-professed role as champion of the working class. Ocasio-Cortez's pushed back on these attacks with a single tweet in which she managed to point out the cluelessness of the "alt-right," specify that clothes worn at shoots are borrowed, reaffirm the candor of her commitment to the working-class, and conclude with the following declaration: "Get used to me slaying lewks because I am an excellent thrift shopper," all within the tweet's 280-character limit. This response alone is emblematic of Ocasio-Cortez's spirited determination to not acquiesce to critics. What followed though provided the Representative an even more compelling opportunity to demonstrate her witty combativeness: conservative news network Fox News created a large video wall graphic that quoted an excerpt of the conclusion to Ocasio-Cortez's tweet alongside a photo from the shoot.

There is little doubt that the Fox News graphic was designed to mock the politician in light of the network's stance on Ocasio-Cortez, already discussed at length in Chapter 5. Yet, as shown in Figure 6.1, Ocasio-Cortez recontextualized the visual within a tweet that included its screenshot and thanked the network for taking the time to make "campaign graphics [she] never knew [she] needed." What was intended by the network as mockery was endorsed by the politician, thereby accomplishing the redirection of the mockery onto the network. We would expect right-wing media to misrepresent or at least negatively portray the political platform of a leftist politician, so Ocasio-Cortez's endorsement of this Fox-News-generated visual is unanticipated, as is her application of a

DOI: 10.4324/9781003273103-6

92 The discursive realization of a 'clapback queen'

Figure 6.1 Reframing criticism in a tweet.

non-serious frame to serious content. Together, these unexpected moves create a humorous effect. This example of interactional reframing works to Ocasio-Cortez's benefit by providing her the opportunity to confront and ridicule attacks to her political persona and to rekey them as baseless and even jocular.

Ocasio-Cortez's ready responses to critic attacks, particularly on social media, have garnered so much attention that an opinion piece in the Washington Post called AOC "a millennial clapback queen" and maintained that she is "as combative […] as one might expect a fed-up former bartender to be" (Emba, 2018). This chapter delves into these responses by reporting on a study of the discursive strategies and stance-taking moves that Ocasio-Cortez employed primarily in her freshman term. It adopts a CDA approach to examine the features that characterize the reframing practices, self- and other-positioning strategies, and stance dimensions in selected responses that she articulated within the remarks she delivered before the US House of Representatives and the tweets she posted in reaction to attacks perpetrated by the media and her political opponents against her and her political platform.

Data and methods

House remarks

The first set of data consists of the remarks Ocasio-Cortez delivered before the US House of Representatives chiefly during her freshman term. It includes the contents of three Congressional hearings of the 116th Congress before the Committee on Oversight and Reform, of which Ocasio-Cortez is a member – "Strengthening ethics" on 6 February 2019, "The need for leadership to combat climate change and protect national security" on 9 April 2019, and "Trump's wrong turn on clean cars: the effects of fuel efficiency rollbacks on the climate, car companies, and California" on 29 October 2019 – which were retrieved from www.govinfo.gov, a website run by the United States Government Publishing Office that provides free public access to official publications from all three branches of the US Government. These instances were purposely selected because they contained imputations and/or recriminations. The first set of data also includes two widely covered responses that Ocasio-Cortez delivered on the House floor: a point of personal privilege (24 July 2020) to address Representative Ted Yoho's remarks and her speech within the censure of Representative Paul Gosar (17 November 2021).

Once the transcriptions were retrieved, the full interactional setting was reconstructed in order to contextualize Ocasio-Cortez's remarks. The stances of the responses by Ocasio-Cortez were then analyzed by identifying stance and style markers, and (re)framing practices (Goffman, 1981), as well as legitimization and self- and other-positioning strategies following a CDA and a broad discourse-historical approach (Reisigl & Wodak, 2001; van Leeuwen, 2007).

Tweets

The tweets analyzed in this chapter were posted by Ocasio-Cortez (using the Twitter handle @AOC) during a roughly 26-month period that began on 26 June 2018, the day of her Democratic primary, and ended on 19 August 2020. The resulting 3,935 tweets (excluding retweets) amounted to a roughly 167,000-token corpus. The corpus was analyzed using the online text analysis tool Sketch Engine first to explore the most frequently used lemmas, or basic words forms, and their original context via the concordance tool. Comparative keyword analysis was also performed against a reference corpus constituted by original tweets from Representatives of the 116th

Congress, developed using the larger corpus created by Wrubel and Kerchner (2020). It includes 30,000 tweets (1,050,262 tokens) posted from 26 June 2018 to 19 August 2020, randomly selected from the larger corpus. This reference corpus was deemed fitting because it comprised tweets posted by US politicians, referred to the same context and timeframe, and used the same variety of English (US English).

A summary of the corpora follows:

- AOC first term: Original @AOC tweets from June 2018 to August 2020 – 3,935 tweets (167,325 tokens)
- Reference: Original tweets from 75 randomly selected Representatives of 116th Congress from 26 June 2018 to 19 August 2020 – 30,000 tweets (1,050,262 tokens)
- Top 40 AOC tweets: 40 tweets with the highest "favorite" (or "like") count from AOC first term corpus – 40 tweets (9,032 tokens)

In order to glean more detailed insights into the stance-taking within Ocasio-Cortez's online communication, a sub-corpus of the top tweets from the larger @AOC corpus was created. To create this sub-corpus, the 3,935-tweet corpus was sorted in ascending order by "favorite" (or "like") count and the top 40 tweets were selected. Several reasons underpin these selection criteria. First, users generally like a tweet because they like its content (Meier et al., 2014) and it is most resonant with and representative of their views, and most-liked tweets are more visible and impactful. Thus, these tweets also convey the reception from the politician's constituents and larger pool of followers and, therefore, are suggestive of the most well-received tweets in the designated timeframe. Second, this amount was selected because 40 tweets represents roughly 1% of the larger corpus. The top 40 @AOC tweets over time were favorited by between 305,684 and 771,335 users (whereas the average like count across all tweets posted by the Representative in the full period under study was roughly 40,000 likes). Although the most-favorited tweets occur throughout the 26-month period, there is a higher concentration of tweets in the summer of 2020.

Stance was analyzed in the sub-corpus of top tweets. First, the stance focus of each tweet was identified. Then, the features that characterize the stance dimensions – affect, investment, and alignment (Kiesling et al., 2018), were explored, with emphasis on (dis)alignment given the aims of the chapter. Once the foci and dimensions were determined and investigated, a CDA approach was adopted for the analysis of the sub-corpus with an emphasis on self- and other-positioning strategies and (re)framing practices (Goffman, 1981) used by the Representative.

"I am incredibly flattered," "This is not about me:" defense, rebuttal, and reprisal on the House floor

The present section examines excerpts of House hearings and debates that present instances in which Representative Ocasio-Cortez acknowledged and responded to criticism and delivered her own reprisals of the opposition in the formal context of the House floor. The analysis proceeds with instances cited in chronological order, to demonstrate an evolution in the Representative's style and scope.

Committee on oversight and reform hearings

In "Strengthening ethics," a 6 February 2019 hearing before the Committee on Oversight and Reform, Ocasio-Cortez questioned Mrs. Karen Hobert Flynn, President of the non-partisan government watchdog group Common Cause about unethical campaign funding practices. At the start of her five allotted minutes, she stated the following:

1 Thank you, Chair. So let's play a game. Let's play a lightning round
2 game. I'm going to be the bad guy, which I'm sure half the room would
3 agree with anyway, and I want to get away with as much bad things as
4 possible, ideally to enrich myself and advance my interest, even if that
5 means putting my interests ahead of the American people. So, Mrs.
6 Hobert Flynn—oh and, by the way, I have enlisted all of you as my
7 coconspirators, so you're going to help me legally get away with all of
8 this. So, Mrs. Hobert Flynn, I want to run. If I want to run a campaign
9 that is entirely funded by corporate political action committees, is
10 there anything that legally prevents me from doing that?

Ocasio-Cortez's discursive aim with the question and its prelude is to demonstrate how easy it is for politicians to rely, unduly and unjustly, on corporate funding for their campaigns, and to delegitimize these politicians and this practice on moral grounds. Although their actions are not illegal, as implied by the question itself, they are positioned as such by using moral evaluations ("bad" lines 2, 3, "putting my interests ahead of the American people" line 5) and the language of criminality ("coconspirators" and "get away with," line 7). Inversely, this argumentation makes it possible for Ocasio-Cortez to position herself on a higher moral ground based on the well-advertised fact that she refuses to accept funding from lobbies.[1]

This serious topic, however, is treated playfully. The Representative begins the prelude to this question by enacting a jocular frame, characterized at once by provocation and playfulness. Ocasio-Cortez achieves this first explicitly by twice inviting the witness to "play a game" and then by assuming of the role of "the bad guy." This jocular effect is intensified by using simple, repetitive lexicon ("the *bad* guy" is defined as someone who wants "to get away with as much *bad* things as possible"), by naming other lawmakers her "coconspirators" (line 7), and by her statement: "I'm sure half the room would agree with" the fact that she is a "bad guy" anyway (line 2). This brief interjection within a playful frame both calls attention to the criticism she has received from her Republican colleagues and makes light of it.

The second instance analyzed comes from an April 2019 hearing in which expert witnesses were heard on the matter of climate change and the Green New Deal – a package of legislation that aimed to address climate change and economic inequality that is Ocasio-Cortez's most renowned policy proposal to date – emerged as a point of debate. Specifically, Republican Representative Clay Higgins from Louisiana delivered a statement in which he expressed climate skepticism and xenophobia but also declared: "I will not criticize my colleague from New York for her enthusiasm and her creativity regarding the Green New Deal." In so doing, Clay associates childlike attributes – or "enthusiasm" and "creativity" – to his "colleague from New York," or Ocasio-Cortez. In contrast with his affirmation that he will "not criticize" his colleague, whom he does not name, the attributive terms he uses are belittling and can be interpreted as an ad hominem attack since they attempt to undermine the validity of the Green New Deal not by critiquing the legislation but by subverting Ocasio-Cortez's credibility, expertise, and competence.

When Ocasio-Cortez takes the floor, she does not immediately reply to this critique. She first asks a series of questions to the expert witnesses, thereby prioritizing climate change. Her response occurs in the last of her five allotted minutes, and follows:

1   You know, I would be remiss if I didn't talk or address some of the
2   comments made across the aisle, and while I am incredibly flattered
3   that the ranking member and many members across the aisle seem
4   to be so enamored with a non-binding resolution presented by a
5   freshman Congresswoman sworn in three months ago, I think that
6   ironically, despite that fixation, it doesn't seem that they've actually
7   read the contents of the proposed and presented resolution. And so
8   I would just – I would encourage that we do not need Cliff Notes for
9   a 14-page resolution that was designed to be read in plain English
10 by the American people. So I would encourage my colleagues to
11 actually read the resolution presented so that they can speak to it
12 responsibly and respectfully.

In her retort, the start of her remark is littered with overstatements and hyperbolic expressions – we see "incredibly flattered" (line 2), "so enamored" (line 4), and even "fixation" (line 6) – which again create a non-serious frame (Haugh, 2010) and serve to mock her opposition. Moreover, by citing both the "non-binding" nature of the Green New Deal (line 4) and her brief tenure as US Representative (line 5), she mitigates and even undermines her authority and her proposed policy again with the effect of mocking her opponents. Adding another layer of jocular mockery, she suggests that the politicians have not even read the resolution in spite of its brevity and simplicity. By citing "Cliff Notes" (line 8), which provide a dumbed-down version of literature, the brief length of the document ("14-page," line 9), its non-specialized language designed for a non-expert audience ("designed to be read in plain English by the American people," lines 9–10), and suggesting that the politicians have not actually read the resolution they criticized ("to *actually* read the resolution," line 11, emphasis added), she implies that her political opponents are slow-witted, indolent, and bigoted. Ocasio-Cortez also suggests that, by opting out of their duties, her colleagues have not acted "responsibly and respectfully" (line 12).

Yet, although Ocasio-Cortez indexes a strong disaffiliative stance, when this retort is analyzed in terms of epistemic positioning strategies, we see examples of subjective and impersonal evidential expressions – or "I think" and "it doesn't seem" (lines 5, 6) – that index an attenuated degree of commitment, or investment. Furthermore, the repeated use of the modal "would" (lines 1, 8, 10), an effective stance marker that attenuates her volition, in the last part of her utterance again serves to mitigate, this time her critique of her opponents.

In the third hearing under study, the 29 October 2019 hearing "Trump's wrong turn on clean cars," Ocasio-Cortez is resolute in her condemnation of politicians who do not endorse or who try to undermine efforts to fight climate change. In the comment reproduced below from this hearing, Ocasio-Cortez responds to an attack directed at her only implicitly because the opposition's actions compromise her environmentalist political platform. The Representative chastises the Republican party for their attempt to adjourn a meeting dedicated to fuel efficiency and organized to criticize the Trump administration's environmental record:

1 Mr. Chairman, may I make a comment? [...] I am--I would like to
2 do my job, and I try not to get out of my job at every opportunity.
3 So given the fact that we have convened the former Governor of
4 California and Senator Whitehouse here, we are here to talk about
5 the very pressing issue of cutting our carbon emissions and saving
6 our planet, and we have an entire political party that is trying to get
7 out of their job, adjourn this hearing, and I just want to know what
8 the reason for such a disrespect of our process would potentially be.
9 Do we have a reason for why this hearing is trying to be adjourned,
10 or, you know, do we have just like a cocktail party?

In this retort, Ocasio-Cortez attacks Republicans by saying that they are evading their responsibilities ("an entire political party that is trying to get out of their job," lines 6–7), again suggesting that they are indolent and lazy. Reminiscent of but more explicitly than in the second excerpt, she condemns her opponents for their lack of respect for their institution ("such a disrespect of our process," line 8). She creates a juxtaposition between the hearing in which a "very pressing issue" (line 5) is discussed that involves "saving our planet" (lines 5–6) and the Republicans' other commitment, dismissed as a "cocktail party" (line 10). Insinuating that the Representatives are trying to adjourn a meeting that discusses issues vital for the well-being of the planet for a social affair is a damning attack that again indexes a strong disaffiliative stance. As in the second excerpt, there is evidence of attenuation of the commitment to this stance with the mitigators "would" (line 8), "potentially" (line 8), "like" (line 10), and the discourse marker "you know" (line 10).

The three excerpts that contain a (counter)attack analyzed thus far suggest that Representative Ocasio-Cortez enacted playful, jocular frames even in the formal context of the House floor. Her playful style crafted an image of herself not as smug and inaccessible but as approachable and even funny. Her lighthearted tone, however, did not diminish the content of her response to her opponents. Rather, notwithstanding evidence of attenuated investment in these claims, she employed this style to infuse biting criticism that positioned her opponents as immoral, acting in their own (and not the American people's) interests, disrespectful of their posts, unintelligent, and lazy. In so doing, the Representative could assign to herself qualities that contrasted this portrayal – morality, productivity, and altruism – and situated her as possessing the qualities of a leader.

A point of personal privilege and a censure vote

On 21 July 2020, the political website *The Hill* ran a story that gained massive coverage for stating that a Republican US Representative from Florida, Ted Yoho, called Ocasio-Cortez a sexist slur at the Capitol building. It reported Ocasio-Cortez's reaction to this event: nothing like this had "ever happened to" her and she "never had" this "kind of disrespect levied at" her (Lillis, 2020). The next day, Yoho took to the House floor to deliver a response. In his speech, he cited his wife and daughters as evidence that he did not use the alleged offensive language. Yoho did not apologize to Ocasio-Cortez nor did he call her by name. Instead, he declared "words attributed to me by the press were never spoken" and "I apologize for their misunderstanding."

The following day, Ocasio-Cortez used a point of personal privilege to address Yoho's remarks on the House floor. An excerpt of this widely covered speech follows:

```
1   ...In front of reporters Representative Yoho called me, and I quote,
2   "a fucking bitch." These were the words that Representative Yoho
3   levied against a congresswoman. The congresswoman that not
4   only represents New York's 14th Congressional District, but every
5   congresswoman and every woman in this country. Because all of us
6   have had to deal with this in some form, some way, some shape, at
7   some point in our lives. I want to be clear that Representative Yoho's
8   comments were not deeply hurtful or piercing to me, because I have
9   worked a working-class job. I have waited tables in restaurants.
10  I have ridden the subway. I have walked the streets in New York
```

11 City, and this kind of language is not new. I have encountered words
12 uttered by Mr. Yoho and men uttering the same words as Mr. Yoho
13 while I was being harassed in restaurants. I have tossed men out of
14 bars that have used language like Mr. Yoho's and I have encountered
15 this type of harassment riding the subway in New York City [...] Not
16 only have I been spoken to disrespectfully, particularly by members
17 of the Republican Party and elected officials in the Republican
18 Party, not just here, but the President of the United States last year
19 told me to go home to another country, with the implication that
20 I don't even belong in America.

In a radical departure from what she stated to *The Hill* reporter, in her address Ocasio-Cortez declares that Yoho's comments were neither "hurtful" (line 8) nor "piercing" (line 8). This, on the one hand, was because she had experienced this type of disrespect countless times before. In this excerpt, she positions Representative Yoho as one of the many men who had "harassed" her (line 13) and his language as a "type of harassment" (line 15), and she cites how she had been "spoken to disrespectfully" (line 16) by House Republicans and former US President Trump. Thus, Ocasio-Cortez relegates Yoho, Republicans, and Trump to the lowly status of men who are "tossed... out of bars" (lines 13–14) for engaging in reprehensible behaviors.

On the other hand, by stating that Yoho's comments were neither "hurtful" nor "piercing," Ocasio-Cortez can circumvent being labeled a victim of an isolated attack. Instead, the event can become emblematic of a wider phenomenon. In this way, this response can be seen as an enactment of an ideational understanding of synecdochal representation[2] (Casullo, 2021), whereby Ocasio-Cortez does not only stand in for every woman (who has experienced harassment), but she is also their leader. According to Casullo (2021), synecdochal representation is a triadic phenomenon that requires a leader to show closeness, charismatic exceptionality, and symbols of power, and these three objectives transpire from this except. With respect to the first, Ocasio-Cortez establishes herself as "of the people" – specifically she mirrors all American women – by stressing the shared nature of this type of experience, reinforced with the use of third person plural pronouns ("all of *us* have had to deal with this in some form, some way, some shape, at some point in *our* lives," lines 5–7), and by naming herself as representative of "every congresswoman and every woman in this country" (lines 4–5). To set herself apart from her followers, she carefully details the extensive experience she has had with this verbal abuse, which helps position her as an authority on the matter and, therefore, brings "authorization" (van Leeuwen, 2007) to the speech, but she also situates her experience as exceptional as it also involves harassment by "members of the Republican Party," "elected officials in the Republican Party," and "the President of the United States" (lines 16–18). With reference to the third objective, she not only cites her institutional role (lines 3–4), but the very act of delivering this speech to the House floor is evidence of the authority and power with which she is vested.

Unlike her responses in the Hearings, in this prepared speech, there is high investment and total commitment toward the information provided. The narrative is constructed in terms of evidential constructions for the evidentiary justification of her viewpoint (Marín-Arrese, 2015) such as "I have worked" and "I have waited tables" (lines 8–9), "I have ridden," and "I have walked" (line 10). These serve to solidify her reputation as a reliable source of information with privileged access to this experience, a stance that is reinforced with expressions of epistemic certainty such as zero-marked modality (Hart, 2011; Marín-Arrese, 2011). Her experiences, institutional role, and credibility grant her legitimacy to condemn the Representative who disrespected her, lay bare a system of oppression, and suggest that she can dismantle this system for all of the women she (synecdochically) represents.

The last response under study is an excerpt from the censure vote of Republican Representative Paul Gosar, in November 2021, who posted an animated video that depicted him slashing Congresswoman Ocasio-Cortez's neck and assaulting President Biden:

1 I have been serving in this body just under three years. In that
2 three years, an enormous amount has happened. But in response
3 to the Republican leader's remarks when he says that this action is
4 unprecedented, what I believe is unprecedented is for a member of
5 House leadership of either party to be unable to condemn incitement
6 of violence against a member of this body. It is sad. It is a sad day in
7 which a member who leads a political party in the United States of
8 America cannot bring themselves to say that issuing the depiction of
9 murdering a member of Congress is wrong, and instead, decides to
10 venture off into a tangent about gas prices and inflation. What is so
11 hard? What is so hard about saying that this is wrong? This is not
12 about me. This is not about Representative Gosar. But this is about
13 what we are willing to accept.

This excerpt, which presents a narrative whose similarity to the aforedescribed incident is uncanny, expresses disapproval of the Republican leader of the House of Representatives for his unwillingness to condemn a reprehensible action toward a colleague. Again, Ocasio-Cortez uses Gosar's actions as a springboard to make a systemwide condemnation. This time, however, Ocasio-Cortez mitigates her role – first implicitly by acknowledging that her tenure as Representative has been short (line 1) and then explicitly by stating that "this is not about me" (lines 11–12). The Republican Representatives' reluctance to censure their colleague's actions takes the foreground, even though the attack was directed at her. The effect of this approach is that it links this event to previous events, most infamously the 2021 United States Capitol attack, it evokes the threat of violence against Congressmembers, and revives nationwide condemnation of that GOP-related event. The third person plural that appears at the end of the excerpt cuts across party lines and, like in the first scripted address to the House floor under study, there is evidence of high investment and commitment toward her affirmations.

In the 2019 hearings, we saw repeated instances of jocular frames and informal language with occurrences of mitigation markers that occasioned an approachable and accessible style that is entirely absent in these latter two examples. In these formal remarks, delivered in 2020 and 2021, there is evidence of an evolution in the Representative's style and scope. Although she displayed evidence of the attempt to represent "the people" synecdochically, her language expresses an increasingly authoritative, national role that is enacted by using forms that express high commitment (and little mitigation) and third person plural pronouns, steering attention to her legitimate authority, and reframing personal attacks as national concerns.

"Don't hate me cause you ain't me, fellas": expressing (dis)alignment on Twitter

The present section shifts focus to the tweets that Representative Ocasio-Cortez posted after her primary win and during her first term as Representative. A general overview of the tweet corpus precedes a closer look at the top tweets.

Frequency and comparative analysis in the AOC first term corpus

To obtain a general snapshot of what Ocasio-Cortez aimed to project on Twitter during her first Congressional term, the full

The discursive realization of a 'clapback queen' 103

Table 6.1 Most frequent lemmas in AOC first term corpus (nouns)

	Lemma	Freq		Lemma	Freq
1	People	826	11	Woman	183
2	Time	299	12	Member	180
3	Community	287	13	Right	167
4	GOP	273	14	Policy	166
5	Today	234	15	Healthcare	161
6	Congress	221	16	Thing	157
7	Year	219	17	Way	154
8	Day	202	18	Worker	153
9	Family	202	19	Life	152
10	Climate	192	20	Power	149

corpus of 3,935 tweets was analyzed for the most frequent lemmas and the top 20 results are shown in Table 6.1. The presence of the terms "people," "community," "family," and "member" evidence the Representative's attempt to establish a sense of belonging, a motif already encountered during her first campaign discussed in Chapter 4.

However, a comparison with the most frequent lemmas in the AOC first campaign corpus (Table 4.1 in Chapter 4) evidences an evolution in the way in which Ocasio-Cortez used the platform as she shifted roles from candidate to Representative. District-based terms that constituted one-quarter of the most frequent lemmas during her campaign no longer figure prominently in the tweets she posted as a freshman Representative, and the lemma "woman" moved up from 19th to 11th position. District-based terms are replaced by terms indicative of her political platform as an environmental activist and democratic Socialist, or "climate," "policy," "healthcare," and "worker," and reference to her political opposition – (the polysemic) "right" and "GOP."

When the corpus was compared to the larger reference corpus of Congressional tweets, further insights are imparted. The top 20 results of the comparative keyword analysis are presented in Table 6.2. Although these results exclude those related specifically to the district (e.g., "Bronx," "NY-14"), which would have, otherwise, been the top results, the absence of the language of belonging that we witnessed in the preceding table is telling. Based on these findings, the community-bound nature of Ocasio-Cortez's language can be deemed endemic to politicians and cannot be considered

Table 6.2 Results of the comparative keyword analysis

Item		Keyness	Item		Keyness
1	GND	120.5	11	Usury	48.8
2	UBI	102.6	12	Alright	48.8
3	Corp	66.8	13	Convo	45.6
4	Marginal	60.8	14	Abt	45.2
5	Waitress	60.8	15	M4A	43.4
6	Organizing	58.7	16	Decarbonize	42.8
7	Runaway	54.8	17	Diff	42.8
8	Outspent	54.8	18	Twitch	42.8
9	Tuition-free	49.7	19	Classist	42.8
10	Pollsite	48.8	20	Neo-nazi	42.8

a unique style. Notable, however, are some terms that the Representative used to describe herself and her campaign, or "waitress," "organizing," and "outspent," which emphasize her humble upbringing, tireless commitment, and self-made success, respectively.

Other keywords are specialized, policy-related terms, including "GND" (Green New Deal), "UBI" (Universal basic income), "marginal" (describing tax rates), "runaway" (describing income gaps), "tuition-free" (for public colleges), "usury" (for high interest rates), "M4M" (Medicare for All), and "decarbonize" (reduce carbon(aceous) deposits). The presence of these terms is both indicative of Ocasio-Cortez's aim to advance her Democratic Socialist and pro-environment political platform and it signals her specialization and expertise, which serves the purpose of legitimating her discourse (van Leeuwen, 2007).

Another category of words that transpires in this comparative keyword analysis is abbreviations, suggesting that Ocasio-Cortez's use of these shortenings exceeds that of her colleagues who use Twitter. These include the policy-related initialisms specified earlier, clippings such as "corp" (corporate or corporation), "convo" (conversation), and "diff" (different), and omissions of the central vowel in "abt" (about). Ocasio-Cortez's use of "alright" can arguably also be considered an abbreviation. This usage suggests command of the Twitter discourse format, given the platform's character limit, but also of informal, online talk. The increased use of these non-standard forms – along with her reference to "Twitch," a popular livestreaming platform for gamers – fashions a style that

The discursive realization of a 'clapback queen' 105

is worlds apart from the traditional, stoic, and institutionalized discourse of leaders. Her style is instead geared toward the construction of a stance of relational closeness with her young followers. Her informal and relaxed language use creates an "audience-centered, rapport-building" style (Johnstone, 2009, p. 39) that crafts a perception of Ocasio-Cortez as young, hip, and media-savvy, and aligned with and alert to the interests of her followers. Furthermore, it marks a continuation in style from her campaign to her first term that establishes her political identity as authentic and coherent.

The top 40 sub-corpus

This section examines a sub-corpus of Ocasio-Cortez's 40 most-liked tweets, which, therefore, resonated the most with her Twitter followers, to uncover what these tweets were about (stance foci) and the types of stances that the Representative took with respect to different topics (stance dimensions).

Stance foci: what the top tweets were about

Twenty-three stance foci were identified in the 40 tweets. Donald Trump, the President and leader of the opposing party when the tweets were authored, and his actions and plans were the most frequent stance foci (ten occurrences), followed by the Republican Party (GOP, five occurrences). Together, the political opposition – including Republican Senator Ted Cruz (one occurrence) and Trump advisor Brad Parscale (one occurrence) – amounted to just shy of half of the stance foci occasioned in the full subset of tweets. Five tweets referred to members of Congress, (the administration of) the United States, and budgets (allocated by legislators), and two tweets targeted her critics in the media, including Fox News host Tucker Carlson. Other issues raised in the tweets included police brutality (two occurrences), women's health issues (three occurrences), race relations (two occurrences), misogyny (two occurrences), and working-class rights (two occurrences). Another common thread was Ocasio-Cortez herself, which accounted for one-eighth of the top tweets, and was manifested in terms of her identity, her political platform and career, and her groundbreaking win.

Given that the most frequent stance foci are Ocasio-Cortez's political opposition, it is unsurprising that the top tweets are characterized predominantly by negative affect. For instance, most negative affect characterized the tweets in which Trump is the focus. Suggestive of this affective stance is the Representative's positioning of Trump as entitled ("A man whose entire life was built on a rich blend of daddy's money and financial fraud [...]," 15 July 2020), evil ("He holds that Bible like it's burning him," 02 June 2020), unfit for office ("This President needs to be impeached," 21 June 2019), corrupt ("Si es Trump, tiene que ser corrupto 💩," 15 July 2020), and treasonous ("a criminal who betrays our country," 04 October 2019).

Only six tweets are characterized by positive affect and, with the exception of a single tweet about essential workers, they are all self-referential. One such tweet, represented below as tweet a), connects Ocasio-Cortez's first primary race to her second, two years later:

a   When I won in 2018, many dismissed our victory as a "fluke."

Our win was treated as an aberration, or bc my opponent "didn't try."

So from the start, tonight's race was important to me.

Tonight we are proving that the people's movement in NY isn't an accident. It's a mandate. 24 June 2020

Although the affective stance toward her victory – alternatingly attributed to herself in the first person singular ("I," "my," "me") and the inclusive plural ("our," "we") – is positive, this positive stance is fashioned in opposition to the derision of her critics, enacted by the use of quotation marks. Indeed, some sort of criticism is embedded even within positive tweets, such that every single one of the most-favorited tweets analyzed contains a covert or overt attack, with the latter far outnumbering the former. Although this analysis is restricted to the top 40 tweets and is not necessarily indicative of her overall Twitter style, it does suggest that her combative approach begets the greatest attention and approval (in terms of "likes").

As a whole, the top tweets authored by Ocasio-Cortez are also characterized by high investment. Not only do the contents of the tweets suggest a high degree of commitment on the part of the author, but there is also little linguistic evidence of hedging devices and uncertainty. In the two brief tweets that follow, the Congresswoman declares what "needs to" happen (b) and what "should not" exist (c):

b   This President needs to be impeached. 21 June 2019

c   The United States of America should not have secret police. 20 July 2020

Neither of these tweets contain devices to mitigate the force of the high-value modal elements, nor do they incorporate linguistic justification for Ocasio-Cortez's commitment to the truth of the proposition. Instead, Ocasio-Cortez's tweets are characterized by "epistemically non-modal" categorical assertions, expressing the strongest possible degree of speaker commitment (Simpson, 2005).

Two more tweets, represented below, display the high commitment of the Representative. While the two tweets refer to different scenarios – tweet d) refers to the death of George Floyd at the hands of police officers while tweet e) responds to Trump's threat to target Iranian cultural sites – they both aim to condemn a crime and, in doing so, follow a similar argumentation structure. To respond to a CNN correspondent's tweet detailing Floyd's autopsy,[3] tweet d) employs the conditional "if x, then y" ("If you killed a man w/ health conditions, you still killed a man"), followed by an account of what occurred to Floyd on the day of his death as evidence of the standpoint. Tweet e) instead begins by framing Trump's plan as "a war crime" following a "y because x" structure (Reisigl & Wodak, 2001), with the standpoint followed by reasoning to support the stance. The tweets both end with a negation – refuting any argument that mitigates or is in support of the antagonists' actions – followed by a final, grave and accusatory affirmation.

d   If you killed a man w/health conditions, you still killed a man. George Floyd couldn't breathe. Three officers held him down, & one w/ a recorded, violent history kneed his neck as others helped. They waited nine minutes for his last breath. This was not an accident. It was murder. 30 May 2020

e   This is a war crime. Threatening to target and kill innocent families, women and children – which is what you're doing by targeting cultural sites – does not make you a "tough guy." It does not make you "strategic." It makes you a monster. 05 January 2020

The argumentation schemes employed by the Representative in these two tweets not only create a rational dispute but also communicate high investment. If, as Kiesling et al. (2018) posit, high investment can be identified with the answer to the question "would [the speaker] defend their claims and opinions to the death?" (p. 713), then the structures of the tweets, careful definition of the crime, rebuff of alternative explanations, and final condemnation suggest that Ocasio-Cortez creates stances of high investment, which are in turn celebrated by her followers in terms of likes.

Lastly, we turn to the analyses of how Ocasio-Cortez aligns with her followers and recriminates opposition policies, politicians, and critics to unveil the strategies through which the Representative constructs and defends her persona and fashions a distinctive style. Over three-quarters (or 31) of the tweets do not have a direct addressee and/or are addressed to a generic, wider audience. Yet, even in these cases the stance focus is the antagonist, and the Representative seems to rally her followers to support her mockery of opponents and recriminations of critics. The tweet that follows provides additional insights:

f   I hear the GOP thinks women dancing are scandalous.

Wait till they find out Congresswomen dance too! 💃

Have a great weekend everyone :) 4 January 2019

A video of Ocasio-Cortez dancing while she was an undergraduate at Boston University in 2010 surfaced and was used by the opposition in the attempt to smear the Representative. The text reproduced in f), along with an 11-second clip, serves as a retort to this attempt. In the clip Ocasio-Cortez light-heartedly yet defiantly points at the camera, performs a light backward shuffle, and lip-syncs to a Motown hit, before bursting into laughter, and exiting the shot by entering in her Capitol Hill office. The subdued dance of a member of Congress in formal attire at the most formal setting of the nation, with a plaque of the Representative's name in plain sight, seems not only to suggest that there is nothing wrong with playful dancing, but it also signals change. Indeed, on the one hand, the tweet and accompanying video, the most liked of the sub-corpus, reaffirms that "women dancing are scandalous" is preposterous. On the other hand, the tweet's youthful, accessible style and playful frame, enacted by the use of emoji and emoticon, the friendly parting phrase with the direct address "everyone," and, above all, by the video, establishes a polar relationship between Ocasio-Cortez and the GOP, where the former is hip and relatable, and the latter is puritan and obsolete.

The remaining tweets, roughly one-quarter of the total, directly address one or more people, and all of these cases represent

The discursive realization of a 'clapback queen' 109

censures. To analyze these instances further, we will take two examples into account. In tweet g), Ocasio-Cortez reprimands the GOP for singling her out during the election of the Speaker of the House. The second phrase constitutes a riposte characterized by several linguistic and semiotic features worthy of exploration. First, it contains non-standard forms, mainly "cause," "ain't,"[4] and "fellas," which occur in non-formal youth talk and African American Vernacular English. "Fellas" underscores the primarily male constitution of the GOP and the woman tipping her hand emoji, commonly used to express sassiness or sarcasm, is modified by skin-tone, placing race as an explicit part of communication (Sweeney & Whaley, 2019). Thus, Ocasio-Cortez distances herself from and disaligns with the GOP not only because she chastises their actions but because her identity is distinct from – and better than – theirs. Specifically, by means of using non-standard forms, and gender and ethnic markers via textual and non-textual features, the Representative both foregrounds her identity as a young, woman of color (WOC) and designates to the GOP the categories old, white, and male.

g   Over 200 members voted for Nancy Pelosi today, yet the GOP only booed one: me. Don't hate me cause you ain't me, fellas 💅
    4 January 2019

h   Sen. Cruz, while I understand you judge people's intelligence by the lowest income they've had, I hold awards from MIT Lincoln Lab &others for accomplishments in microbiology. Second, I'm surprised you're asking about chromosomes given that you don't even believe in evolution. 28 February 2020

Tweet h is a reply to Republican Senator Ted Cruz's condescending response to Ocasio-Cortez's tweet criticizing the Trump administration's choice of head to the US coronavirus response effort, which read as follows: "As you are speaking as the oracle of science, tell us, what exactly is a Y chromosome?" 27 February 2020. Unlike Cruz's response, in tweet h), Ocasio-Cortez explicitly names the Senator, and includes his title. She cites her accomplishments to construct an authoritative stance and to discredit his sarcastic remark but does so after a dependent clause in which she positions Cruz as a classist. Then, instead of replying to what may be seen as a misogynist reference (i.e., the chromosome that determines the male sex), Ocasio-Cortez affirms that Cruz is an evolution denier as a recriminatory resource. In short, Ocasio-Cortez delegitimates and disaligns from Cruz based on his science skepticism and her science-based experience.

The final two tweets under study rely heavily on visual cues as pivotal accompanying information, so they are be presented as screenshots (Figures 6.2 and 6.3). Indeed, the most telling component of tweet i) is the visual, by cartoonist Will McPhail that has a caption (not pictured) that reads: "Describe what you can bring to this company." (Figure 6.2). Ocasio-Cortez sets her experience with House Republicans as comparable to the image in the comic, in which a female candidate is interviewed by ten white, middle-aged males. Once again, the lack of diversity in the GOP is made manifest.

Tweet j), instead, takes aim at critics of her first primary win. Ocasio-Cortez labels the demographic rationalization of her victory over Joseph Crowley as "false" outright, citing having won with "voters of all kinds" as evidence. The only reason the candidate (and her team) won – emphasized by the explicitly stated "period" – is her hard work, which she had occasioned throughout her campaign. The image of the deeply worn shoes reframes the statement "I knocked doors until rainwater came through my soles" from a hyperbole to an authentic account. By inviting readers to "respect the hustle" she asks that the role her work ethic and agency played in her win be acknowledged.

With this retort, Ocasio-Cortez authenticates her candidacy and situates herself in the tradition of American success stories. Hard

Figure 6.2 Screenshot of tweet i).

The discursive realization of a 'clapback queen' 111

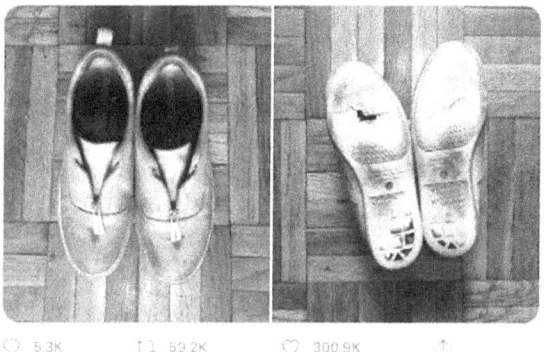

Figure 6.3 Screenshot of tweet j).

work and dedication evoke the all-American "work ethic" trope that dates back to the Puritans and colonial times. By appealing to this deeply entrenched theme, Ocasio-Cortez positions herself among archetypal, successful Americans who have pulled themselves up by their own bootstraps. The attached photographs support this even more firmly. Democratic presidential nominee Adlai Stevenson's hole in the sole of his shoe was famously depicted in a 1952 Pulitzer-prize winning photograph and, more recently, Barack Obama's worn soles were the protagonists of a famed 2008 photograph by Callie Shell. This tweet, therefore, both verbally and visually reverberates the message that Ocasio-Cortez, a force to be reckoned with, fits well within the historical tradition of American leaders, and embodies the producerist ideal.

The comparative keyword analysis of the full corpus of tweets posted by Ocasio-Cortez from 2018 to 2020 revealed several words that accentuated her humble upbringing, tireless commitment, and self-made success, and these same themes emerged in the analysis of her attempts to create stances of alignment with her followers and disalignment with her opposition. In addition, evidence of the rapport-building style that transpired in the analysis of the full corpus was also present in the top tweet sub-corpus, most visibly in her astute use of emoji, emoticons, and visuals. However, it was her expressions of most negative affect with respect to her adversaries and her high investment, enacted by "epistemically nonmodal" categorical assertions (Simpson, 2005) and argumentation schemes, that cast Ocasio-Cortez's online discourse as committed, powerful, and genuine. Furthermore, her stances of disalignment with the political opposition and critics paved the way to forge her political identity in contrast with the out-of-touch, obsolete, and bigoted white, male GOP.

Conclusions

The analysis in this chapter has shown both divergences and convergences in Ocasio-Cortez's discursive strategies and stance-taking employed to impute stances of (dis)alignment based on her audience and the communicative platform she uses. In the Committee hearings analyzed, which all occurred in the year in which the Representative was sworn into office, Ocasio-Cortez used non-serious frames in her disalignment from and mockery of her opponents, even at the risk of undermining her own authority. In her critique of her colleagues, she weakened the strength of her "clapback queen" persona with stance markers that attenuated her commitment and mitigated her antagonistic stance. As these were the only responses that were less scripted and were delivered orally before her adversaries, it is unsurprising that her investment was diminished in these ways.

In the formal remarks delivered in 2020 and 2021 within a point of personal privilege and a censure vote, the Representative's style and scope shifted. Serious frames, expressions of high commitment, third person plural pronouns, and attention to her legitimate authority fashioned an increasingly authoritative tone. In both instances, the Representative rescaled attacks that were directed at her as concerns common to a large proportion, if not the totality, of the American people. The effort to downplay her response to and/or role in the experience at hand – or Yoho's sexist slur and Gosar's posted video – did not redirect the spotlight. Rather, it strengthened her position of expertise, authority, and leadership by, for instance, enacting all three objectives of synecdochal representation, which is a powerful means of populist performance (Casullo, 2021), and situating her in the long line of political activists and leaders in the American tradition.

On Twitter, stances were constructed with her opponents through the use of an informal and relaxed style, presented with emojis, shortenings, and non-standard forms that served not only to show alignment with her Bronx- and Queens-based constituents but also to portray herself as someone who is a skilled and authentic code-switcher across diastratic and diaphasic varieties. Humor used alongside ad hominem attacks enacted mockery and/or recast the target of mockery, and, like in the Committee hearings, rekeyed the frame from serious to jocular. These linguistic devices positioned her as youthful, in-touch, and relatable. Boulomaic modality – expressing wishes and desires of speakers recurrent in political discourse – was virtually absent from this sample of tweets. Instead, Ocasio-Cortez's tweets were characterized by epistemically non-modal categorical assertions, expressing the strongest possible degree of speaker commitment (Simpson, 2005).

Admittedly, the choice to analyze multiple instances likely jeopardized the depth of analysis and this is a limitation of this chapter. This notwithstanding, more than one context and audience allows us to see how versatile the expression of stances within (counter)attacks can be. Even within one individual who has become so strongly associated with combative responses – i.e., "clapback queen" – we see evidence of mitigation and attenuation in more formal contexts in which this type of talk is expected. These different contexts suggest that Ocasio-Cortez was nimble in her responses to attacks and criticism, and as the argumentative nature of the top-liked tweets suggest, this may be the root of her popularity. Her agility and deftness in drawing on the different tools at her disposal across communicative channels provides evidence of what has made the political communication of newcomer politicians such as Ocasio-Cortez effective and newsworthy. Indeed, these defensive discourses served to maintain her authenticity and legitimacy, to safeguard the coherence of her personal narrative and political self, and to situate herself within a larger national and historical storyline.

Notes

1 Her 158-character Twitter bio includes "People-Funded, no lobbyist 💰".
2 To stress the power of populist performance, Casullo (2021) explains that a populist leader's followers believe that "the very persona of the leader embodies their own identity, not in an ideational but in a concrete, physical way" (p. 75), which she calls synecdochal representation. Importantly, my analysis here presents a departure from Casullo's focus on the physical body of the populist leader, which is one of the points discussed in my analysis of Ocasio-Cortez's political ad (Chapter 4).

3 The 29 May 2020 tweet written by CNN Correspondent Shimon Prokupecz (@ShimonPro) read as follows: "Important from autopsy: The combined effect of George Floyd being restrained by the police, along with his underlying health conditions and any potential intoxicants in his system likely contributed to his death, according to the criminal complaint."

4 The presence of 'ain't' in this tweet is particularly poignant in light of the criticism that she would receive just four months later for her use of the contraction during Al Sharpton's National Action Network Convention in New York.

References

Casullo, M.E. (2021). Populism as synecdochal representation. In P. Ostiguy, F. Panizza & B. Moffitt (Eds.), *Populism in Global Perspective* (pp. 75–94). New York-London: Routledge.

Censuring Representative Paul Gosar, 116th Cong. (2021). https://www.govinfo.gov/content/pkg/CREC-2021-11-17/pdf/CREC-2021-11-17-pt1-PgH6336.pdf

Emba, C. (2018). Alexandria Ocasio-Cortez is appealing because she's real. Can she keep it that way? *Washington Post*, Retrieved from: https://www.washingtonpost.com/opinions/alexandria-ocasio-cortez-is-appealing-because-shes-real-can-she-keep-it-that-way/2018/11/25/ce779a0e-ef4b-11e8-96d4-0d23f2aaad09_story.html

Goffman, E. (1981). *Forms of Talk*. Philadelphia: University of Pennsylvania Press.

Hart, C. (2011). Legitimising assertions and the Logico-Rhetorical module. *Discourse Studies,* 13(6), 751–769.

Haugh, M. (2010). Jocular mockery, (dis)affiliation, and face. *Journal of Pragmatics,* 42, 2106–2119.

Johnstone, B. (2009). Stance, style, and the linguistic individual. In A. Jaffe (Ed.), *Stance: Sociolinguistic Perspectives* (pp. 29–52). Oxford: Oxford University Press.

Kiesling, S.F., et al. (2018). Interactional stancetaking in online forums. *Computational Linguistics,* 44(4), 683–718.

Lillis, M. (2020). 'Ocasio-Cortez accosted by GOP lawmaker over remarks', *The Hill*, Retrieved from: https://thehill.com/homenews/house/508259-ocaasio-cortez-accosted-by-gop-lawmaker-over-remarks-that-kind-of.

Marín-Arrese, J.I. (2015). Epistemicity and stance: A cross-linguistic study of epistemic stance strategies in journalistic discourse in English and Spanish. *Discourse Studies,* 17(2), 210–225.

Marín-Arrese, J.I. (2011). Epistemic legitimizing strategies, commitment and accountability in discourse. *Discourse Studies,* 13(6), 789–797.

Meier, F., et al. (2014). More than liking and bookmarking? Towards understanding Twitter favouriting behaviour, *Eighth International AAAI Conference on Weblogs and Social Media*.

Question of Personal Privilege, 116th Cong. (2020). https://www.govinfo.gov/content/pkg/CREC-2020-07-23/html/CREC-2020-07-23-pt1-PgH3702-2.htm

Reisigl, M. & Wodak, R. (2001). *Discourse and Discrimination: Rhetorics of Racism and Antisemitism.* London: Routledge.

Simpson, P. (2005). *Language, Ideology, and Point of View.* London-New York: Routledge.

Strengthening ethics: Hearing before the Committee on Oversight and Reform, 116th Cong. (2019). https://www.govinfo.gov/content/pkg/CHRG-116hhrg35793/html/CHRG-116hhrg35793.htm

Sweeney, M.E. & Whaley, K. (2019). Technically white: Emoji skin-tone modifiers as American technoculture. *First Monday,* 24(7), n.p.

The need for leadership to combat climate change and protect national security: Hearing before the Committee on Oversight and Reform, 116th Cong. (2019). https://www.govinfo.gov/content/pkg/CHRG-116hhrg36439/html/CHRG-116hhrg36439.htm

Trump's wrong turn on clean cars: The effects of fuel efficiency rollbacks on the climate, car companies, and California: Hearing before the Committee on Oversight and Reform, 116th Cong. (2019). https://www.govinfo.gov/content/pkg/CHRG-116hhrg38306/html/CHRG-116hhrg38306.htm

van Leeuwen, T. (2007). Legitimation in discourse and communication. *Discourse & Communication,* 1(1), 91–112.

Wrubel, L. & Kerchner, D. (2020). 116th U.S. Congress Tweet Ids, *Harvard Dataverse*, V1.

7 The identity work of a modern leader

Introduction

The case of US Congresswoman Alexandria Ocasio-Cortez was chosen for this book about the construction, presentation, and dissemination of political identities because her political ascent was truly noteworthy in its nature and outcomes. She is not the first young political aspirant who swiftly pulled off an upset win and who gained widespread coverage: she has shared the stage with other Progressive members of "the Squad" whose rise bore semblance to her own in their vociferous opposition to the former US President. However, AOC – her extensively used nickname – has been embraced as the new face of the Democratic party and she has commanded the attention of the US media in a way that is comparable only to Trump.

In broad terms, this book has tasked itself with exploring how Ocasio-Cortez achieved this feat. Much of the attention that she has garnered has centered on the way in which she has communicated with her constituents, with the American people, and with her critics, and the exploration into this political communication has been the focus of the present work. Specifically, it has hinged upon three different perspectives, to which each of the following sections is dedicated: the construction, the challenge to, and the defense of a newly realized political identity.

Narrating a new political identity

Political campaigns strive to create narratives that present, promote, and position a candidate both within a logical timeline and an ideologically coherent worldview (Meade & Robles, 2017). They articulate the reasons for which a candidate is running for political office and discursively justify why she or he should be in office.

DOI: 10.4324/9781003273103-7

The identity work of a modern leader 117

The development of coherent and consistent personal narratives is, of course, particularly pivotal for candidates who are not yet widely known in the popular political landscape. Ocasio-Cortez was once such candidate when she embarked on her first campaign for the NY-14 seat of the US House of Representatives in 2017. Two of the means through which the candidate built and disseminated her narrative were her campaign advertisement, *The Courage to Change,* and her tweets. Through these means, she presented and affirmed to her constituents an image of a candidate who is an ordinary, authentic, working-class New Yorker, a member of the NY-14 community, and a champion for "the people."

One of the main messages that Ocasio-Cortez advanced in her campaign was that she was an ordinary person. In her campaign advertisement, the video-style technique lacked luster and the camera shots did not glamorize the candidate. The visuals intentionally focused on mundane acts such as getting ready for work in a small New York City apartment, slipping out of flats into heels on a subway platform, visiting a local bodega, and taking public transportation. The candidate was also shown fulfilling more official functions such as speaking to small groups of constituents, canvassing a neighborhood, working alongside campaign volunteers, and speaking to a large audience, but the video ended with an intimate family dinner, again inside an apartment. The visual narrative was one of an ordinary citizen who does ordinary things, but she is trying to tackle a noteworthy feat: obtaining political victory as an actual representative of the district.

The identity work that fashions Ocasio-Cortez as an ordinary person and an actual representative of NY-14 involved more than showing her engaged in run-of-the-mill practices and through non-glamorous frames. What it means to be representative of the district was explicitly defined by the voiceover of the video, spoken by the candidate herself: she is a woman, not affluent, of Puerto Rican descent, and of the working class. The fact that these identity categories were all occasioned in the first 37 seconds of the two-minute video not only accentuated the multifaceted nature of Ocasio-Cortez's identity, but it also positioned her identity at the forefront of her campaign. It was at the heart of why she should be in office, and why her opponent Joseph Crowley should be voted out.

This effort was contingent on presenting an impregnable narrative of the candidate's membership in and closeness to her district and its constituents. This was achieved in the visual story told in her video that strove to convey that she was representative – and even emblematic – of her community. It was also achieved within the tweets she authored during her campaign. One of the most palpable ways in which Ocasio-Cortez indexed her insider identity was via implicit and explicit mentions of Puerto Rico (PR), her Puerto Rican heritage, and the perceived concerns of the Puerto Rican community. Evidence of this transpired throughout the analyses of the campaign tweet corpus. One of the most frequently used words in her tweets was "community," and the analysis of the collocational behavior of this term revealed that she associated "community" primarily with "Latino" and "immigrant" populations who were "underserved" and "under-repped" by their government officials. The comparative keyword analysis unveiled significantly more references to the PR and to policies and issues that directly affected this community, such as the "PROMESA" (Puerto Rico Oversight, Management, and Economic Stability Act) and Hurricane María, to a greater extent than other Representatives during the same time frame. Furthermore, her use of the acute accent (i.e., María), Spanish words (e.g., "hermana"), frequent use of the flag of Puerto Rico emoji, and choice of skin-tone modified emoji acted as both visual identity markers that positioned Ocasio-Cortez as a member of the Latinx and Puerto Rican communities, which constituted roughly 50% and 10% of the district population, respectively (US Census Bureau, 2019), and as cohesive devices that reinforced the credibility and authenticity of her projected identity.

The status as insider of NY-14 was also achieved by Ocasio-Cortez by accentuating that she was a Washington outsider. On the one hand, this was manifested within the content of the tweets themselves: the candidate condemned the practices, legislation, and funding policies of her incumbent adversary, in particular, and of the establishment, in general. These tweets that displayed indignation at her opponent and the wider system mentioned her adversary by name, and used emoji to highlight her message (such as the money bag emoji to stand in for corrupt money). They also contained evidence of the quintessentially populist "us" versus "them" construction. In her campaign ad, Ocasio-Cortez proclaimed "This race is about people versus money. We've got people, they've got money," which referred literally to her access to volunteers instead of compromising, corporate money, but it figuratively connected the candidate to the people whose unanswered demands were familiar – because she is connected to the community – and were her own – because she is "one of us." In contrast, her opponent was a profiteer who did not even "drink *our* water or breathe *our* air."

Therefore, he "cannot possibly represent *us*." Presenting herself as an ordinary person itself implied that she was of "the people" and not a member of the elite. Her most frequently used word in the tweet corpus was in fact "people," a word that was associated with young, non-elite (or "everyday people"), workers, and/or part of the working class. By describing her opponent as a spendthrift outsider to the community who had only been concerned with his own self-aggrandizement in his tenure as Representative, Ocasio-Cortez situated Crowley as a member of "the elite" establishment. The juxtaposition between a NY-14 insider (herself) and the Washington establishment (Crowley) was a pivotal strategy in the delegitimization of her primary opponent on the grounds that he did not know and/or was not acting in his constituents' best interests.

Ocasio-Cortez's yearning to appear as a Washington outsider was also evinced by the distinctive style that characterized her tweets compared to other candidates and lawmakers. For instance, her emoji use far exceeded that of other Representatives, and only the dollar sign ($) and the percentage sign (%) were used more frequently, in absolute terms, in the reference corpus of Representatives' tweets that was over eight times larger than Ocasio-Cortez's campaign corpus. She adopted the purple heart emoji as a symbol of her brand and as her signature, used emoji as identity markers (such as the PR flag and skin-tone modified emoji), and inserted emoji to emphasize critical points (such as corrupt money that she does not accept). In addition to their use as devices to achieve coherence and emphasis, use of emoji was an emblematic resource that presented the candidate as digitally savvy, approachable, and youthful.

The narrative Ocasio-Cortez crafted during her first campaign was carefully constructed, discursively and multimodally, to be at once cogent and authentic by drawing on textual and non-textual resources. It was characterized both by traditional political discourse and great innovation to achieve, for instance, an effective new mode of enacting the language of (left-wing) populism (Kazin, 2017). It also fashioned a style that positioned her as young and approachable, reinforced her campaign brand, and naturalized the link among her race, her past, and her will to embody and fight for her community.

Subverting the narrative

Fox News, the mainstream bastion of conservative and right-wing populism, relentlessly covered Ocasio-Cortez, a young, popular, rising star with a Democratic Socialist platform since her primary win and subsequent freshman term in the US House of Representatives. This coverage aimed to undercut the coherence, trustworthiness, and soundness of the narrative that Ocasio-Cortez so carefully realized during her first campaign.

The analysis of the ten most viewed Fox News segments dedicated to Ocasio-Cortez revealed several mechanisms by which network hosts, anchors, and guests strove to delegitimize the lawmaker. First, Fox News hosts evoked the threat of terrorism and authoritarianism in their censure of Ocasio-Cortez's actions and beliefs. In so doing, they warned their audience that the Representative could – inadvertently or deliberately – stunt national development, seize private property, silence dissenting views, and hurt millions of Americans. These warnings could be read as cautionary tales in which Ocasio-Cortez is the un- and/or anti-American antagonist who quashes American ideals and subverts the well-being of the American people. This portrayal runs counter to Ocasio-Cortez's narrative of ally of the people against the corrupt elite.

Furthermore, Fox News coverage contained negative references and predications that framed the Representative as mentally deficient, illogical, unintelligible, ignorant, and uninformed to cast doubt on her intelligence, rationality, and acumen. They also called attention to her age, inexperience, and marital status to portray her as ill prepared and incompetent. Ocasio-Cortez did not make grand claims concerning her education, preparation, or political experience in the narrative that she crafted in her campaign, but these verbal attacks on her personality and character undermined the authority, expertise, and credibility with which Ocasio-Cortez was vested as an elected official and lawmaker. The Fox News coverage was teeming with personal attacks against the Representative in response to her opinions and policies, which, therefore, constituted fallacious *argumentum ad hominem* (Reisigl & Wodak, 2001).

Perhaps the greatest threat that Fox News posed to the strength and coherence of Ocasio-Cortez's campaign narrative was by presenting a compelling, dissenting narrative in which the media, Bernie Sanders, and political advisor Saikat Chakrabarti orchestrated her campaign and election, and were "the brains behind" the Green New Deal, her most famous pieces of legislation. Not only does this narrative give rise to conspiratorial suspicions of nefarious aims of concealed actors, but it also wholly invalidates the story that Ocasio-Cortez told that running for Congress "wasn't in the plan" and the compulsion to undo the damage of her spendthrift predecessor drove her into politics. The insinuation that she was chosen and groomed nullifies the authenticity and credibility of her political identity as an ordinary American, a representative of the people, and a member of her community whose central aim was "to fight for a New York that working families can afford," as stated in her campaign ad. In addition to situating her and her trajectory as fraudulent, this rewriting of her narrative designated her as a powerless pawn.

The analysis of the processes that governed the decontextualization of Ocasio-Cortez's words and their recontextualization onto a segment of "Tucker Carlson Tonight" showed how the Fox New host manipulated the Representative's words and message to enact his own "preferred reading" for the discourse (Blommaert, 2020). The use of increasingly shorter soundbites from political communication has characterized US television news for decades: as Hallin (2021) explains, we have moved from a time "when television news transmitted the words of political leaders with little editing or interpretation to one in which they cut those words up to weave them into narratives and interpretive frameworks, which they would articulate for their audiences." (p. 50). In the news segment under study, the Fox News host distorted the Representative's words and message entirely by backgrounding (and foregrounding) selected elements, adding gestures and evaluations, and applying parodical frames.

Closer analysis of this segment provided the opportunity to delve into the nexus between right- and left-wing populism. Evidence of right-wing populist references and sentiments could be found across segments in the form of "us" versus "them" dichotomies, appeals to the moral convictions of producerism, and instancing of traditional gender roles, but Tucker Carlson[1] – more so than any host – referenced nationalist and xenophobic ideologies indicative of right-wing populism chiefly in his responses to Ocasio-Cortez's pro-immigrant stance. Throughout this widely viewed segment, Carlson discredited the Representative's arguments within soundbites that included emotionally charged language and expressed the pathos of the tragic (Ostiguy & Moffitt, 2021) – quintessentially populist characteristics – by framing her as whiny, authoritarian, and anti-American. At the end of the segment, Carlson mocked the Representative for dismissing factual and semantic accuracy in favor of moral righteousness. Yet, the performance of affinity with lay epistemic culture where outrage trumps expertise, credentials, and empirical evidence is a central tenet of the cultural populism of

Fox News (Peck, 2021). The Representative's dismissal of facts and accuracy is in line with the network's approach to appeal to emotions over facts and to their tendency to reduce coverage to insults. The analysis of these widely viewed Fox News segments revealed the discursive strategies that were used in the delegitimization, other-presentation, and recontextualization of the Representative and her claims, but another layer was heeded to examine the effects of this coverage: or how the messages of the videos were negotiated, re-oriented, and re-entextualized in YouTube comments. YouTube commenters frequently referred to Ocasio-Cortez's mental deficiency and intellectual incapacity, in line with Fox News coverage, but also included vulgar and misogynist epithets that expressed sexist stereotypes to which Fox News hosts alluded. Thus, although the comments were highly vitriolic, vulgar, and offensive, they maintained and only amplified the message contained in the mainstream coverage of the Representative. Moreover, commenters re-oriented their remarks to a larger scale and occasioned discourses of right-wing populism, nationalism, xenophobia, and Islamophobia, which provides evidence that this space – sanctioned by a mainstream media outlet on a social media platform – facilitates the circulation and reinforcement of exclusionary and discriminatory ideologies.

Safeguarding the narrative

Representative Ocasio-Cortez has not cowered silently in response to the criticism that she has received. On the contrary, the replies to this criticism have constituted a pivotal means by which the political identity that she constructed in her primary campaign has been reinforced and consolidated.

The present work has analyzed responses to criticism in impromptu responses, scripted questions, and prepared statements delivered in official activities at the Capitol building and in the tweets that the Representative posted onto her personal account. The imputations and recriminations contained within answers Ocasio-Cortez delivered during three hearings before the Committee on Oversight and Reform in 2019 demonstrated that the Representative enacted playful, jocular frames even in the formal context of the House floor. The frames allowed her to make damning attacks of her opponents – including that they are immoral, selfish, slow-witted, indolent, and bigoted – while retaining an affable and reachable persona. This style also helped her strengthen her image

The identity work of a modern leader 123

as a "Bronx girl" and an ordinary person ready to fight the elite to obtain the demands of the people.

The more scripted responses delivered to the House floor as a point of personal privilege and within a censor vote displayed linguistic evidence of greater commitment via expressions of epistemic certainty such as zero-marked modality. In the former, which occurred in the summer of 2020, the Representative scaled up a single name-calling event and presented it as an instance of an endemic problem that affects all women. Her experience before and since taking office was occasioned as evidentiary justification to her viewpoint that was expressed with epistemic certainty. Her institutional role, explicitly named at the start of her response, granted her legitimacy on authoritative grounds to condemn the Representative who disrespected her, expose a system of oppression, and suggest that she can dismantle this system. In the latter, which was delivered a year and a half later in response to a video posted by a Republican Representative which depicted Ocasio-Cortez's murder, Ocasio-Cortez also rescaled this instance as indicative of a larger issue of lacking accountability for grievous acts. While Ocasio-Cortez took a different approach than the former instance and deflected the limelight by referring to her brief yet eventful tenure and explicitly stated that "this is not about me," she turned the reflectors on the GOP and House leadership. She censured their reluctance to condemn the lawmaker's actions but used language reminiscent of other events, or the 2021 US Capitol attack. Thus, this personal instance became an opportunity for the Representative to chastise the opposition, to remind the people of one of the most infamous events in recent US history, to depict them in a bad light, and to situate herself in opposition to them, as moral and righteous.

The tweets that Ocasio-Cortez posted during her first Congressional term were also analyzed. Once she was elected Representative, Ocasio-Cortez tweeted less about her district and more about her platform and the opposition party than she did when she was a candidate. When compared to tweets posted by other Representatives who used the platform in the same period, the tweeted narrative that transpired highlighted reference to her Democratic Socialist and pro-environment political platform as well as the terms "waitress," "organizing," and "outspent," which emphasized her humble upbringing, tireless commitment, and self-made success. Importantly, this comparison also revealed that the Representative used a lot of initialisms and omissions in her tweets, which, of course, are helpful to respect the platform's character limit, but these linguistic devices deviate from formal communicative norms and expectations and, therefore, reinforce Ocasio-Cortez's image as young, hip, savvy, and "one of us," and establish alignment with her followers.

A closer look at the top 40 most liked tweets revealed that roughly half were about the political opposition, and all but six tweets were characterized by negative affect. This suggests that Ocasio-Cortez attracted the most positive attention from her followers when she chastised the opposition. The top tweets were further characterized by evidence of high investment on the part of the author as well as little linguistic evidence of hedging devices and uncertainty. Importantly, they also pointed to her persona as a clapback queen, which further consolidated her identity as a populist and her discourse as populist because "it fits populism's triumphant narratives and tirades against opponents" (Tumber & Waisbord, 2021, p. 18).

In summary, her responses to attacks have served to accentuate the onslaught of attacks that she has endured, laying bare the sexist and classist ideologies embedded therein. Moreover, Ocasio-Cortez has launched her own offensive against the opposition, through which she strove to maintain her authenticity and legitimacy, to safeguard the coherence of her personal narrative and political self, and to present herself not as a freshman politician but within a larger American national and historical storyline. Her high investment, playful frames, and rapport-building style have not only powered her popularity and exposure but have also served to solidify, reinforce, and embellish the political persona that she sketched – in opposition to the out-of-touch, bigoted white male GOP – as an authentic Bronx-born member of the working class and paladin for the people.

Looking ahead

As a social media-savvy millennial woman of color who was suddenly catapulted into the political scene, the discursive realization of Ocasio-Cortez's political persona has been unexpected in terms of its divergence from traditional approaches. Ocasio-Cortez evolved from political unknown to legitimate threat to the political status quo of the United States. Since taking office, Alexandria Ocasio-Cortez has solidified, reinforced, and embellished the political persona she sketched during her candidacy as an authentic community member and paladin for the people, and one of the most resounding ways in which she has accomplished this is by responding to attacks.

The identity work of a modern leader 125

As the youngest female US Representative in American history, since January 2019, Ocasio-Cortez has not veered from her narrative. She condemned actions by the Trump administration that threatened social justice, and she has taken a vociferous stand against powerful businessmen, most notably the CEOs of Facebook and Amazon, thereby chastising "the elite" of political, economic, and media realms. The Representative's calls for direct constituent participation via these networks – such as when she crowdsourced questions for Mark Zuckerberg on Twitter in October 2019 – can be interpreted as a shift toward a more immediate relationship between the people and their leaders. Ocasio-Cortez's tweets written in reply to Trump's discriminatory comments garnered hundreds of thousands of likes from her Twitter followers. Representative Ocasio-Cortez's House Remarks in response to Yoho were covered globally and the C-SPAN video of these remarks has been viewed over 3 million times on YouTube.

Her painstakingly curated social media presence, discussed at length in the present book, is replete with personalization, and her remarkable social media clout is representative of her amplified reach and popularity. At the time of writing, her followers reached 13 million on Twitter and 8.5 on Instagram. She even joined TikTok in 2021. In light of this, one of the main limitations of this study was, in fact, that Twitter was the primary source of data. Although the importance of Twitter in today's political discourse is undeniable, Twitter offers only a limited picture of today's complex media ecology (Jungherr, 2016). Heed of these multiple channels and the new media tools employed by candidates can create more a representative, comprehensive, and updated picture of political communication and they should be investigated in future studies.

For her sophomore run for election, the campaign video entitled *A Better World is Possible* was posted to her Twitter account on 18 June 2020 with the accompanying message:

> A better world is not only possible, it is within our reach.
>
> From mutual aid in our communities to solidarity in the streets, the people of New York have already started to reshape our future.
>
> It's time to bring the movement to the voting booth.
>
> VOTE this Tuesday, June 23rd.

Although Ocasio-Cortez has secured widespread notoriety that she did not possess when *The Courage to Change* was released, similarities exist in the contents of the first video and the message that frames the second. First, reminiscent of her slogan "It's time for one of us" in *The Courage to Change*, Ocasio-Cortez situates herself as a community-member with the use of first-person plural pronouns. Then, she deemphasizes her role as Representative and her responsibility for gains achieved ("mutual aid in our communities to solidarity in the streets") and attributes these gains to "the people of New York" rather than her and her team, again foregrounding "the people" (arguably, over money). Like in her previous video in which she urged that "A New York for the many is possible," this message frames her electoral win as a movement. The video itself, which as of May 2022 amassed 6.9 million views on Twitter, however, is leaps and bounds away from the original video. *A Better World is Possible* begins with Ocasio-Cortez speaking directly to the camera as she walks confidently along a street in her district and defines, in unmitigated terms, the issues that plagued New York in 2020. Just the first five seconds of the campaign video embody Ocasio-Cortez's progression from political unknown to one of the most recognizable American lawmakers, and what this implies for how her political identity is enacted.

This book was chiefly about *how* the narrative of a single politician who has come to emblemize contemporary political discourse – of course adopted and coopted from and shaped by other politicians – and what it means to be a bootstrapping American progressive and left-wing populist was fashioned, challenged, and defended. This, however, was just the start of the story. Alexandria Ocasio-Cortez's career has only just begun, and this influential politician will undoubtedly inspire not only many politicians to follow in her footsteps but also researchers to investigate her political discourse, which given her know-how has been and will likely continue to be deeply influenced by the wide-ranging affordances and challenges presented by the age of social media.

Note

1 Tucker Carlson's populist rhetoric concerning the protection of the welfare of an ethnically defined (i.e., 'European, Christian, and English-speaking') 'people' from 'illegal' immigrants and the ruling class is discussed in Chapter 2.

References

Blommaert, J. (2020). Political discourse in post-digital societies. *Trabalhos em Linguística Aplicada*, 59(1), 390–403.

Hallin, D.C. (2021). Rethinking mediatisation: Populism and the mediatisation of politics. In H. Tumber & S. Waisbord (Eds.), *The Routledge Companion to Media Disinformation and Populism* (pp. 49–58). London-New York: Routledge.

Jungherr, A. (2016). Twitter use in election campaigns: A systematic literature review. *Journal of Information Technology & Politics*, 13(1), 72–91.

Kazin, M. (2017). *The Populist Persuasion: An American History*. Ithaca-London: Cornell University Press.

Meade, M. & Robles, J. (2017). Historical and existential coherence in political commercials. *Discourse & Communication*, 11(4), 404–432.

Ostiguy, P. & Moffitt, B. (2021). Who would identify with an "empty signifier"? In P. Ostiguy, F. Panizza & B. Moffitt (Eds.), *Populism in Global Perspective* (pp. 47–72). New York-London: Routledge.

Peck, R. (2021). 'Listen to your gut': How Fox News's populist style changed the American public sphere and journalistic truth in the process. In H. Tumber & S. Waisbord (Eds.), *The Routledge Companion to Media Disinformation and Populism* (pp. 160–168). London-New York: Routledge.

Reisigl, M. & Wodak, R. (2001). *Discourse and Discrimination: Rhetorics of Racism and Antisemitism*. London: Routledge.

Tumber, H. & Waisbord, S. (2021). Media, disinformation, and populism: Problems and responses. In H. Tumber &S. Waisbord (Eds.), *The Routledge Companion to Media Disinformation and Populism* (pp. 13–26). London-New York: Routledge.

US Census Bureau, 2019. Congressional District 14 (117th Congress), New York Retrieved from: https://www.census.gov/mycd/?st=36&cd=14

Appendix

Spoken words and visual images of the first 37 seconds of Alexandria Ocasio-Cortez's first political campaign advertisement, *The Courage to Change*.

Line	Spoken words (nondiegetic)	Visual images
1	Women like me aren't supposed to run for office.	{fades in, from behind} Woman faces mirror, head bowed, ties her hair. Medium shot of part of reflection of candidate's face; a window and AC unit also in view {low angle shot of building}
2	I wasn't born to a wealthy or powerful family.	{from side} Woman turns on bathroom light {from behind} Candidate's reflection is in view in bathroom mirror, applying makeup
3	Mother from Puerto Rico, dad from the South Bronx.	{from behind} Candidate walks up stairs to exit building {zooms out from parents' photograph; steady shot of photograph of father and baby}
4	I was born in a place where your zip code determines your destiny.	{medium shot} Candidate is on platform as subway pulls into station {close up} Candidate sits in subway, turns to look out window {Moving image of buildings, houses, subway}
5	My name is Alexandria Ocasio-Cortez.	{from behind} Candidate exits subway station {from front} Candidate walks along street, looks right and smiles before looking down

(*Continued*)

130 *Appendix*

Line	Spoken words (nondiegetic)	Visual images
6	I'm an educator, an organizer, a working-class New Yorker.	{from front} Candidate speaks to people in garden {from the side} Candidate speaks to woman on street {from side} Man pours coffee
7	I've worked with expectant mothers, I've waited tables, and led classrooms.	{from back} Man mows park lawn {from front} Candidate speaks to expectant mother {from side} Candidate takes a cupcake and laughs with kids at bake sale
8	and going into politics wasn't in the plan.	{from behind, centered} Candidate walks along street {from front and below} Candidate smiles slightly, gazes upward, continues walking

Index

Note: **Bold** page numbers refer to tables and page numbers followed by "n" denote endnotes.

Abreu, R. 47
abstraction 30, 66, 78, 82
additions: as recontextualizing principle 31, 66, 78, 79
adequation 25, 41, 42, 44, 59
affect *see* stance
alignment *see* stance
argumentation: as discursive strategy 5, 65, 73, 82, 83, 107, 112
arrangement: as recontextualizing principle 31, 66, 80
authentication 25, 39, 41, 43, 60, 110
authorization: as legitimization category 28, 29, 65, 67, 71–77, 101, 102; as tactic of intersubjectivity 25, 41

Bauman, R. 30
Blommaert, J. 9–10, 31
bodega 48, **56**, 57, 117
Brand New Congress (BNC) **56**, 57
Briggs, C.L. 30
Bronx 2, 41, 46, 47–48, 49, **50**, 51, 55, 56, 58, 59, 103, 113, 123, 124, **129**

Carlson, T. 18–19, 66, 67, 70, 72, 73, 74, 77–81, 83, 88n10, 105, 121, 126n1
chain of equivalence 18
Chakrabarti, S. 75–76, 83, 120
climate change 79, 93, 96, 98; and skepticism 26, 79, 96; *see also* Green New Deal

Clinton, H. 13
CNN 107, 114n3
Committee on Oversight and Reform 93, 95, 122
comparative keyword analysis *see* keyword
concordance 40, 47, 49, 50, 51, 67, 85, 86, 93
Constitution (US) 15
context 30, 31, 32, 33, 64, 65, 81, 94, 95, 99, 113, 122; and DHA 5–6
coronavirus 109
corpus-assisted discourse studies 3, 6
critical discourse analysis (CDA) 3, 4–6, 7n1, 11, 13, 17, 28, 29, 30, 65, 92, 93, 95
Crowley, J. 2, 43–44, 53, 54, 56, 59, 110, 117, 119
Cruz, T. 105, 109
cultural populism 18, 81, 121

delegitimization 10, 23, 27–32, 64, 65, 67, 71, 72, 73, 77, 82, 85, 95, 119, 122; and multimodality 29–30
Democratic socialism: political platform 2, 43, 57, 59, 103, 104, 120, 123
denaturalization 25, 41
Discourse-Historical Approach (DHA) 5–6, 65, 93
distinction: as tactic of intersubjectivity 25, 41, 44

Index

emblematic resource 24, 25, 52, 91, 119
emoji 51–56, 57, 58, 59, 61n4, 108, 109, 112, 113, 118, 119; and skintone modified 53, 56, 60, 109, 118, 119
entextualization 30, 31; *see also* re-entextualization
existential coherence 23, 27, 44, 75

Facebook 29, 33, 34, 125
Fairclough, N. 5, 30, 65
Floyd, G. 107, 114n3
footing 33, 41
Fox News populism 9, 17–20, 64, 70, 81, 121–122
frames 33, 41, 58, 59, 70, 81, 82, 83, 92, 96, 108, 113

Gee, J. 5, 24
GOP **50**, 54, 77, 102, 103, 105, 108, 109, 110, 112, 123, 124
Gosar, P. 93, 101, 102, 112
The Green New Deal 75, 79, 96, 97, 104, 120

Hannity, S. **66**, 68, 69–70, 83
healthcare 103; and immigration 70
Higgins, C. 96
historical coherence 23, 27, 69
Hobert Flynn, K. 95
Hurricane Maria 55, 57, 61n5, 118

ICE *see* US Immigration and Customs Enforcement (ICE)
identity: construction 24, 25, 33, 58; performance 24, 25; work 24, 42, 44
illegitimation 25, 41, 44, 48, 63
indexicality 4, 33
Instagram 78, 125
intensification: as discursive strategy 5, 65, 75
investment *see* stance

Jackson, A. 15
Jeffersonianism 15
Justice Democrats (JD) 1, 57

Kazin, M. 14–16
Kennedy, J.F. 13

Kennedy, T. 2
keyness 56, 67, 88n11, 104; and analysis 67, 84–85
keyword 40, 57, 67, 88n12; and comparative keyword analysis 40, 56, 57, 67
Ku Klux Klan 15

Laclau, E. 14, 16, 18
Lahren, T. **66**, 72
left-wing populism 2, 15, 39, 57, 119, 121, 126; and discourse 3, 4, 17, 20, 60

McCain, J. 58
McPhail, W. 110
Medicare for All 104
mitigation 5, 65, 102, 113
moral evaluation 28, 29, 65, 73–74, 81, 95
mythopoesis 28, 29, 65, 67, 68, 71, 79, 82

N-gram 67, 86
nomination: as discursive strategy 5, 65, 72
NY-14 38, 42, 43, 44, 46, 48, 49, 51, 56, 58, 91, 117, 118, 119

Obama, B. 1, 11, 12, 29, 111
Omar, I. 63, 85

Parscale, B. 105
Peck, R. 17–18
Pelosi, N. 2, 109
The People's Party 15
perspectivization 5, 65
Pirro, J. **84**, 85, 87
populist rhetoric 17, 18, 19, 81, 126
positioning theory 23, 24–25, 41
predication: as discursive strategy 5, 65, 72, 80, 82, 86, 120
presence: as recontextualizing principle 30, 65, 78
Pressley, A. 63
producerism 15, 18, 54, 70, 77, 83, 111, 121
Puerto Rico 51, 52, 54, 55, 56, 57, 118, **129**

Puerto Rico Oversight, Management, and Economic Stability Act (PROMESA) 55, **56**, 57, 118

Queens 2, 46, 47, 49, 53, 56, 113

racial nationalism 15
rationalization 28, 29, 65
Reagan, R. 68, 69
recontextualization 23, 29, 30–31, 64, 65, 77–82, 83, 87, 91, 121, 122
recontextualizing principles 30, 65
re-entextualization 23, 31, 84, 87, 122
relationality principle 25
right-wing populism 4, 15, 64, 79, 83, 119, 121: and discourse 3, 17, 19, 20, 64, 122; ideology 71, 73, 87
Roosevelt, F.D. 68, 69

Sanders, B. 2, 11, 15, 75, 83, 120
Shapiro, B. **66**, 69, 73, 74, 87n6, 88n9
stance 23, 32–34; and affect 33, 94, 105–106, 124; alignment 33, 94, 98, 108–111, 112, 124; focus 33, 94, 105, 108; investment 33, 94, 97–98, 99, 101, 102, 106–108, 112, 124; object 32, 33
Stevenson, A. 111
style 32–33, 34, 57–58, 60, 93, 95, 99, 102, 104–105, 108, 111, 112, 119, 122–123, 124; *see also* Twitter

synecdochal representation 100, 112, 113n2

tactics of intersubjectivity 25, 41
TikTok 125
Tlaib, R. 63
Trump, D. 1, 2, 4, 13, 15, 18, 20, 47, 48, 58, 61n1, 63, 85, 93, 98, 100, 105, 106, 107, 109, 116, 125
Twitch 104
Twitter 1, 26, 34, 39, 40, 45, 47, 56, 57, 59, 60, **66**, 78, 93, 102, 104, 112, 125, 126; and bio 113n1; followers 105, 125; fundraiser 46; for political communication 12–14; style 106

Universal Basic Income (UBI) 104
US Capitol attack 102, 123
US Immigration and Customs Enforcement (ICE) 48

van Dijk, T. 5, 27
van Leeuwen, T. 28, 29, 30, 65

Watters, J. **66**, 72, 75–76, 86, 88n9
Wodak, R. 5, 30
work ethic (Protestant) 15, 54, 71, 110, 111

Yoho, T. 63, 93, 99–100, 112, 125
YouTube 12, 20, 64–65, 66, 67, 84–87, 122, 125

For Product Safety Concerns and Information please contact our EU representative GPSR@taylorandfrancis.com
Taylor & Francis Verlag GmbH, Kaufingerstraße 24, 80331 München, Germany